PREPPER'S ARMED DEFENSE

**Lifesaving Firearms
and Alternative
Weapons to Purchase,
Master and Stockpile**

Jim Cobb

Ulysses
Press

Published in the US by:
Ulysses Press
P.O. Box 3440
Berkeley, CA 94703
www.ulyssespress.com

ISBN: 978-1-61243-561-9
Library of Congress Control Number: 2015952136

Printed in the United States by United Graphics Inc.

10 9 8 7 6 5 4 3 2 1

Acquisitions editor: Keith Riegert
Managing editor: Claire Chun
Editor: Renee Rutledge
Proofreader: Lauren Harrison
Index: Sayre Van Young
Front cover design: what!design @ whatweb.com
Interior design: Jake Flaherty
Cover artwork: bullets © bezikus/shutterstock.com; stungun © Ari N/shutterstock.
    com; target © alexskopje/shutterstock.com; pepper spray © Adrin Shamsudin/
    shutterstock.com; knife © Jim Cobb; gun safe © Miguel Garcia Saavedra;
    background texture © LeksusTuss/shutterstock.com
Interior artwork: see page 170

Distributed by Publishers Group West

For Tammy,
I may never get you your piñata full of bunnies but I'll see
what I can do about a couple of baby goats.

CONTENTS

INTRODUCTION

Before you begin Chapter 1, I want you to have a full and complete understanding of what this book is and what it is not.

This book will not teach you all you need to know in order to become lethal with the weapon(s) of your choice. There is no book, website, or video series that can do so. Proficiency only comes with practice.

This book will not improve your marksmanship with a firearm. Again, that only comes with copious amounts of range time.

This book will not turn you into a super-soldier on par with John Rambo, Jack Reacher, or Mack Bolan.

What this book will do is show you all sorts of tools for doing harm against your fellow man. It will tell you the pros and cons for each weapon and, hopefully, help you determine which ones might be best for you. The hard stuff, the actual work involved with training, practicing, mastery, is up to you.

It is a sad fact that we live in a violent world. It would be wonderful if every day was filled with rainbows and sunshine, and every human being you met had nothing but good intentions. Unfortunately, that just isn't the case. There are some truly awful people out there who would harm you and your loved ones for no other reason than to see your expression change.

I've tried in vain to track down the source of this quote; it sums up rather well how I feel about learning self-defense techniques: "It is better to be a warrior in a garden than a gardener in a war." In other words, it is preferable to know how to defend yourself and never need to do so than to be in a bad situation and not have a clue what to do about it.

Weapons are tools, nothing more. They are not inherently evil. They can't move on their own; they can't fire themselves. The intention behind their use comes from the user. Weapons serve to increase the speed and power of our defense.

Pretty much everything you're going to read in this book is geared toward hurting another human being. There's no way around it, so let's tackle it head on. We're talking injuries, disfigurement, pain, and even death. I am providing the information contained herein for educational purposes only. What you choose to do with the information rests on you and you alone.

Always seek out proper training with regard to any weapon you choose to use. Doing so will go a long way toward preventing self-injury. Used properly, a weapon may save your life. Used improperly, it could end your life.

Laws vary from place to place. It is up to you to do the necessary research to determine if a given weapon or tactic is legal in your jurisdiction and whether there are any restrictions related to the weapon or tactic. What is legal in my state might not be legal in yours and vice versa. Furthermore, every situation is different. The facts in each case are unique.

I am not an attorney. Nothing in this book may be construed as legal advice in any way, shape, or form. When seeking legal advice, please speak with a licensed and competent attorney, ideally one you've paid with actual money and with whom you have a retainer agreement. Asking your friends on Facebook for their input is not an acceptable substitute.

Reader discretion is advised. The weapons and tactics discussed herein will at times be accompanied by graphic descriptions of injuries. While I will refrain from including illustrations of the damage that can be caused through the use of the tactics, methods, and weapons discussed in this book, consider this fair warning that I'll be discussing blood, lacerations, dislocated joints, broken bones, and worse.

The information discussed herein consists solely of discussion points. I make no recommendations other than the use of common sense in applying what is discussed here to your particular situation. The weapons, tactics, and methods of self-defense outlined in this book may work for some, but not for all. Every person comes to the table with different physical and mental capabilities, levels of experience, and backgrounds. A weapon or tactic successfully used by one person may fail for the next, owing to a variety of factors.

CHAPTER 1

THE REALITIES OF SELF-DEFENSE

As with most things, self-defense in the real world is far different from what you see on the silver screen. Confrontations are often loud and are always stressful. They can turn violent in the blink of an eye. Many people have given thought as to exactly how they'd respond to an attack. However, when a physical conflict does happen, those plans often go flying out the window. Forget all about some sort of Jackie Chan maneuver using a couple of potted plants and a ladder to take out six attackers at once. German Field Marshal Helmuth von Moltke wrote, "No plan of operations extends with any certainty beyond the first contact with the main hostile force." This has often been paraphrased as, "No battle plan survives first contact with the enemy."

Whether you are armed or unarmed, a confrontation typically happens without warning and is over quickly. There are exceptions, of course, but as a general rule, they are finished in seconds, not minutes. The aftermath, however, can last a lot longer and include such things as trips to the hospital or court battles, not to mention potential psychological effects like nightmares and anxiety attacks.

Expect to be injured, even if you prevail. Prevailing over your attacker and remaining unscathed would be miraculous in most cases. The exception to that would be in situations where you were armed, particularly with a firearm, and the other person was either unarmed or was not able to effectively deploy their weapon. Otherwise, expect to be bloodied. The most important thing is that you're still on the green side of the grass come the following morning.

SITUATIONAL AWARENESS

Staying safe begins way before any physical confrontation comes to pass. In fact, the ideal to strive for is never needing to use your weapon(s). Both common sense and situational awareness will reduce or eliminate the number of times you get into trouble.

Situational awareness is simply taking off the blinders and paying attention to the world around you. Keep your head up and your eyes open, watching for potential threats as you go about your day. This doesn't mean you need to be paranoid, afraid to even walk out your front door. It just means you need to stop updating your social media accounts every seven seconds and focus on the real world instead of a screen. Criminals look for those they perceive as easy targets. If you show a confident appearance, keeping your chin up and your head on a swivel, muggers and other ne'er-do-wells will find cause to look elsewhere.

Common sense is part of this, too. Don't put yourself in situations that carry a high risk of going south on you. Avoid dark, unfamiliar alleys at night. When feasible, don't walk alone. Stay out of the bad parts of town if you're able to do so. Keep your vehicles locked up, even when you're at home. Keep your doors at home locked, too. Avoid doing things that will make you an easy target. Crooks are generally pretty lazy. They want the easy score and will almost always choose a target that looks timid, unaware, or weak. Practicing strong situational awareness will take you out of those categories immediately.

TRAINING IS CRUCIAL

I don't care what weapon you decide to carry. If you aren't experienced with its use, if you haven't practiced or trained with it, your odds of being successful plummet drastically. You need to know how to employ the weapon in a range of situations, including in good and bad weather conditions, on your feet, and from the ground.

Ten minutes of waving a knife around in your apartment while you pretend to be some sort of low-rent ninja isn't going to cut it, no pun intended. Seek proper training from a qualified instructor, whether you're considering a firearm, blade, or bludgeon. Know your weapon's strengths, weaknesses, and limitations. This isn't the sort of thing you'll pick up by reading a couple of books or watching a few YouTube videos. You're going to have to get off your butt and venture outside, as scary as that might sound.

WHAT TO DO AFTER THE CONFRONTATION

The confrontation is over and you prevailed. Now what? Here's some advice on what to do in the following scenarios:

You've used a firearm on a home intruder. The intruder or attacker is down for the count. You need to make two phone calls as soon as possible. One of the calls is to your attorney and the other is to 911, not necessarily in that order. When calling the authorities, provide your name and location, and request for both police and rescue squad units to be dispatched. There is no need to go into elaborate detail with the dispatcher as to what happened. Just stick to the salient facts, such as reporting a gunshot victim who needs assistance. Do not go into detail on how the person got shot or who shot him. Do, however, give them a detailed description of what you look like and what you're wearing. This will allow responding officers to identify you quickly and, hopefully, not mistake you for a bad guy.

Unless you firmly believe danger is still imminent, holster or otherwise secure your weapon. When the officers arrive, immediately put your hands in the air to show they are empty. Respond to all directions quickly. Remember, while you know what happened, they do not. Expect a little rough treatment until they get things sorted out. It is in your best interests to comply with all instructions. Now is not the time to argue about self-defense or whether this was a righteous shooting. In fact, discuss the event as little as possible until you have an attorney at your side. That said, I strongly advise you to be polite and respectful to all responding law enforcement officers. This would be a very bad time to get mouthy or snotty. Despite all of their training and experience, officers are only human. As such, they are just as subject to stress and emotion as the rest of us. Responding to a call where they know going in there are weapons involved is not generally seen as a fun time. Tensions will be running high for all involved. Do what you can to reduce the anxiety rather than fan the flames, so to speak.

Allow yourself to be checked out by the responding emergency medical personnel. Adrenaline and shock can do funny things to your body, and you could be injured, even seriously, without realizing it. Have all wounds thoroughly cleaned, especially when there may be a danger of contamination from bodily fluids such as blood or saliva.

You've used a firearm on a home intruder. The intruder has escaped through the back door and fled. First, do what you can to ensure the intruder has truly left the scene. If there is a window that overlooks the direction of his

LEGAL REPRESENTATION

If you are involved in any sort of violent encounter that will eventually involve the police, you will want an attorney on your side. Few of us actually have attorneys on retainer for legal matters that might crop up, of course, but many people have an attorney they've used for this, that, or the other thing. Even if they don't routinely handle domestic shooting incidents, they may be able to help you find an attorney who does. The important thing is to get the ball rolling with legal representation as quickly as possible.

Listen to your attorney and follow their directions, especially when it comes to volunteering information to the police. While you want to cooperate with them and provide them with as much information as possible to help them locate and apprehend your attacker, you also don't want to incriminate yourself if you've inadvertently broken the law during the confrontation.

One of the best things you can do is to sit down with an attorney who is experienced in such matters and have them explain what you can and cannot do under the letter of the law when it comes to self-defense at home as well as when you're out and about. As you go through these scenarios, you'll find the instruction to call an attorney at some point in each case.

flight, use that to observe the area. Avoid walking out the same door he used, just in case he's lurking immediately outside of it. If you have neighbors close by, gather your family together and head over there, then call the police.

Home invaders often work in teams, and there may be someone else in your home who you haven't seen yet.

When you call the police, tell them there was an intruder and give as detailed a description of the person as possible. The dispatcher will ask for the intruder's direction of travel as well as whether they were armed or not. Be sure to tell the dispatcher where you are and what you look like so as to avoid confusion when the officers arrive. Then, call your attorney.

As mentioned earlier, most incidents are over very quickly. Depending upon the state and local statutes in force in your location at the time of the incident, you may find yourself embroiled in a much longer battle, this one involving the court system.

SELF-DEFENSE LEGAL CONCEPTS

Remember, I'm not an attorney and nothing in this chapter or book should be construed as legal advice. That said, I felt it would be prudent to address a few legal concepts related to armed self-defense. If nothing else, consider this more incentive to do your own research and carefully consider any situation prior to employing defensive measures.

ADRENALINE RUSH

One way the body reacts to stressful situations, particularly those involving perceived or actual danger, is with an adrenaline rush. During an adrenaline rush, the adrenal gland dumps hormones called epinephrine and norepinephrine into the bloodstream. These hormones cause the heart rate to speed up and blood vessels to open wider. Airways also dilate, allowing for an increase in oxygen to the lungs. All of this serves to make you a little stronger and faster. Plus, your sense of pain will be somewhat dulled.

Once the danger is over and those hormones are burned off, don't be surprised if you feel shaky and nauseous. Both are very normal reactions and will pass with a little time. Deep, calming breaths and a little walking may help.

Concealed carry. As it stands currently, there are four categories or types of policies when it comes to concealed carry laws in the United States.

1. **Shall issue.** The state allows for concealed carry and requires some sort of license or permit to do so. The requirements for obtaining the permit or license are spelled out in the law and are relatively easy for most people to meet. For example, requirements can include paying a fee or passing a class.

2. **May issue.** The state allows for concealed carry and requires a permit or license, but the issuance of the permit or license is at the discretion of the issuing agency, such as the police or sheriff's department. In other words, there is a degree of leeway as to who gets a license and who doesn't.

3. **Unrestricted.** The state allows for concealed carry and does not require any sort of license or permit for doing so.

4. **No issue.** The state does not allow for concealed carry by private citizens.

As of this writing, the majority of states fall into the "shall issue" category. Many of those states will also recognize the licenses issued by other states. There are restrictions in some places as to the size or caliber of firearm allowed to be carried or what other weapons are permitted.

Of course, the question is, what does concealed carry mean? In a general sense, if a weapon is carried in such a way that it cannot be easily seen by the naked eye, it is considered concealed. Stuffing a handgun in your waistband and draping your shirt over it would obviously be concealed carry. In some states, if the weapon is in a holster and the holster is at least partially visible, it is not considered concealed.

Laws vary widely across the country. Do yourself a favor and research the laws in your area thoroughly so you know what is and what is not allowed.

Deadly force. Generally speaking, deadly force refers to actions taken that one may reasonably presume will cause serious bodily harm or death to the subject. Shooting someone in the chest or stabbing them in the neck with a knife would all be considered deadly force. Those are pretty obvious examples.

It is important to remember that even non-lethal means of defense can turn deadly. An expandable baton can seriously damage someone's cranium just as easily as it can be used to restrain someone. A lot has to do with intent, particularly what's referred to as "evidence of intent."

Sticking with the example of the expandable baton, let's say you get behind your assailant and are attempting to restrain them by holding the baton across their chest. As they struggle, the baton rises up their body, eventually going across their throat. In the heat of the moment, you don't realize this until they've slumped to the floor. Your intention was merely to restrain them until the police arrived, but you inadvertently strangled them during the struggle.

On one hand, your actions and crime scene analysis would make your intention clear. However, it would be difficult to argue an intention of restraint if, when the police arrived, you were still washing blood, hair, and brains from that baton because you bounced it off your attacker's skull a dozen or so times after they were already down for the count.

As a matter of course, deadly force is generally warranted only in situations where you honestly and truly fear great bodily harm, sexual assault, or death will befall you or another person if you don't take action.

Castle doctrine. Castle doctrine is a legal principle that often comes into play in matters of self-defense. The basic idea is that your home is your castle, and as such, you should be free to protect yourself and your family while there. Naturally, because this is a legal issue, there's a lot more involved, but that's the basic gist.

Castle doctrine isn't a law in and of itself, but rather a legal concept around which laws are written or formed. Each state differs as to how it interprets or uses castle doctrine in its laws. I highly recommend doing your own research on how your state's judicial system has interpreted castle doctrine over the years. Case law, meaning actual cases that have been tried using the applicable laws, go a long way toward clarifying muddy or confusing issues.

Castle doctrine typically works like this: If someone unlawfully enters your home *and* you as the occupant believe your life or the lives of your family members are in immediate danger of physical harm or death *and* you've done nothing to provoke or encourage the intruder to enter the home or attempt to harm you or members of your family, you are within your legal rights to defend yourself using force up to and including that of the deadly variety.

Let me break that down a bit. First, pay attention to the word "unlawfully," as it is pretty important. If a member of law enforcement is acting lawfully, say serving an arrest warrant, castle doctrine doesn't come into play. The same may apply in some landlord/tenant situations. If, for example, your lease allows for the landlord to enter the dwelling after giving sufficient notice, and the landlord enters the home after giving such notice, he or she is likely acting in a lawful manner.

Second, the word "reasonable" often comes into play. For example, it might be used thusly: "If a reasonable person were to believe their life to be in immediate danger, then deadly force is acceptable." What is or is not reasonable can be rather subjective, and it is best to err on the side of caution. Be absolutely certain of not just your target but your target's intentions toward you and your family.

Third, note the part about provocation. Castle doctrine isn't applicable if, say, you run outside, bonk someone on the head for no legal reason, than flee back into your house. While the person you bonked might enter your home unlawfully, as in without permission, and they most certainly may mean to cause you harm, you started it, so, at least in a legal sense, you may have to take your lumps or accept responsibility for your actions.

Duty to retreat. Some states, rather than focusing on castle doctrine, utilize what has been termed "duty to retreat." In those states, in order to legally employ deadly force, the victim of the attacker or intruder must have reasonably felt he or she had no other options available. In other words, the person employing deadly force must have either attempted to flee or felt that fleeing would place them in even more danger.

Quite often, castle doctrine trumps this duty to retreat if the incident occurs at the person's home or, in some cases, their workplace or vehicle. Again, do your homework so you have a solid understanding of the laws that apply in your state.

Stand your ground. In other states, there is no duty to retreat and, instead, citizens are legally allowed to stand their ground. Basically, as long as you're not acting in the commission of a crime and you are legally allowed to be where you are at the time of the incident and you truly believe you are in danger of great harm or death from an assailant, you are legally allowed to use deadly force without having to attempt to retreat or flee first.

CRIMINAL VERSUS CIVIL LAW

There are two basic types of law—criminal and civil. This is a huge oversimplification, but criminal law is the side that involves the police and civil law is the side that involves lawsuits.

Castle doctrine and the related legal principles previously outlined typically concentrate on the criminal end of things. Basically, castle doctrine is considered a valid defense against criminal charges related to the incident. It doesn't necessarily mean you cannot be charged with a crime. It just means that you have a legal defense against such charges should they arise. This is provided, of course, that your actions are in line with what is legally allowed in your state with regard to self-defense.

Many castle doctrine statutes also address the possibility of civil lawsuits stemming from the incident. Specifically, the statute might provide immunity against lawsuits being filed against you by the family of the intruder whom you rendered motionless in your back hallway. Now, bear in mind that here in the United States, someone can file a lawsuit against another person for just about any reason you can imagine. Filing suit doesn't mean they are going to prevail, of course, but it still might end up costing you money in attorney fees to get the case dismissed.

• • •

Suffice it to say that if you're involved in an incident where force is used, your first phone call should be to 911 and your second call should be to a competent attorney.

CHAPTER 2

NON-LETHAL SELF-DEFENSE OPTIONS

Despite what keyboard warriors will tell you online, there is indeed a place for non-lethal self-defense options. When you get down to it, the whole point of self-defense is to make sure you're still alive and kicking come the next morning. If blinding an attacker with pepper spray so you can get away accomplishes that, I don't see a problem with it.

In fact, non-lethal options are often preferable to the deadly alternatives, at least from a legal standpoint. In many areas, carrying lethal weapons such as firearms or knives isn't allowed without a permit, if at all. A non-lethal option is far better than having nothing at all to protect yourself.

Law enforcement officers have to comply with the use of force continuum. This is basically a step-by-step guide detailing how much force may legally be used against someone else in different scenarios. The use of force continuum is a standard that applies to everyone in the agency or department. The exact steps will vary from department to department as no universal standard exists here in the United States, but lethal force is always at the far end of the spectrum, with several levels of force preceding it. The steps leading up to lethal force include verbal commands, using joint manipulation techniques, pressure points, kicks, punches, and then the use of some of the weapons discussed in this chapter, such as pepper spray and electronic devices.

The basic idea is to avoid choosing the lethal option immediately unless the circumstance truly warrants doing so. In some cases, deadly force may well be the only viable choice, such as when faced by an intruder armed with a firearm. In other situations, though, a non-lethal approach may be a far better option. Plus, you stand much less chance of being charged with a crime or having to defend yourself from a lawsuit if your assailant is still breathing.

Non-lethal weapons also have a place with those who don't feel they could truly use a deadly weapon, even if their life or the lives of their loved ones were at stake. Whether due to religion or otherwise, some people just

NON-LETHAL VERSUS LESS-THAN-LETHAL

As you shop around for some of the products I'm going to discuss, you may run into the term "less-than-lethal" rather than "non-lethal." For the intents and purposes of this book, these terms are interchangeable. I'm using "non-lethal" simply because it means less typing for me. Any weapon, indeed virtually any object, can be a lethal weapon with enough imagination and ingenuity. We designate certain weapons as non-lethal or less-than-lethal simply because they were not designed to be deadly when used as intended.

Non-lethal weapons are designed to incapacitate the assailant in some way so you can either get away or otherwise prevent them from harming you. These weapons may still cause serious injury, even when used as designed. Caution is advised.

don't feel killing is ever justified. If that's the case with you, then this chapter has your name written all over it.

As with all other weapons discussed in this book, check your local laws so you know what is allowed and what is verboten. Even non-lethal weapons have been the subject of intense legislation in many areas.

PEPPER SPRAY

Pepper spray consists of a mixture of capsaicin and water that is pressurized into an aerosol spray. Capsaicin is the active ingredient. This is the same compound that gives chili peppers their bite. Pepper spray is sometimes called OC spray. OC stands for "oleoresin capsicum," which boils down to mean an extract from one or more plants, such as chili peppers, in the *Capsicum* genus.

The effects of pepper spray are immediate. The eyes slam shut and begin tearing. Breathing comes in fits and coughs. The skin burns, too. Rubbing the eyes only makes matters worse. Without treatment, these effects last at full strength for 30 to 45 minutes. If you can't get away from an assailant with half an hour of lead time, you are doing something seriously wrong.

Pepper spray

Strength

Pepper spray is an extremely effective deterrent, so much so that it has been adopted for use by law enforcement and military agencies. That's the good news. The bad news is that the pepper spray industry is largely unregulated. This means that the quality control isn't consistent across the board.

OC percentage. As you shop around for pepper spray, you'll see most manufacturers advertise the percentage of

OC in their spray, such as 10 percent. That's all well and good, but it is essentially meaningless. All they are telling you is how much OC is in the spray, which has little to nothing to do with the heat level of the spray. OC can be made with dozens of different types of peppers, some obviously hotter than others.

SHU rating. Many manufacturers will mention a Scoville heat unit (SHU) rating for their pepper spray. This is at least a little more information than just the OC percentage. The Scoville scale measures the amount of perceived heat in peppers. Ratings run from 100 SHUs or so for a banana pepper to around 350,000 SHUs for a habanero pepper to 1,500,000 SHUs for a Carolina Reaper pepper. The problem with using SHU ratings for pepper spray is while the OC being used might be rated quite hot, it could be diluted in the mixture so as to keep manufacturing costs down.

CRC measurement. The most reliable method for comparing relative heat among different types of pepper spray is to look for the CRC measurement. CRC stands for "Capsaicin and related Capsaicinoids" and is a measurement of how much of the OC is actually capsaicin. The Environmental Protection Agency (EPA) actually monitors this very closely and this is about as close to regulated as the pepper spray industry gets. Look for a CRC measurement of at least 1 percent.

Delivery System

Always check the package or product description to determine the delivery system, such as a spray, a fog, or a stream. The latter is far preferable as it not only allows you to better aim the chemical into your assailant's face, but there is less chance of blowback from windy conditions. The last thing you want is to blast yourself in the face.

A relative newcomer is the gel delivery system. This type of delivery system is very accurate and has the bonus of being very sticky. There are also foam pepper spray products on the market that work similarly.

Avoid the fog types if possible. These often end up just as dangerous to the user as they are to the intended target. Even a slight breeze can send that cloud right back at you.

One other option that is related to the delivery system is the addition of a dye to the spray. The idea here is that the target will be readily identifiable to the authorities even after the immediate effects of the spray have diminished. This is definitely a desirable feature.

Range

Be sure you fully understand your chosen product's effective range. Each product and delivery system will have a different range. More focused delivery systems, like a stream or gel, tend to have a longer range than others.

It isn't enough to know your product's range is, say, 15 feet. Can you accurately estimate that distance? Grab a tape measure and head outside. Draw a circle to represent the effective range of your spray, with you at the center of the circle. Without looking at their feet to see when they cross into the circle, have someone walk toward you. Try to guess when they are in range and see if you're right. Have them come at you from different angles (hence, the circle). Do this repeatedly until you get a good feel for it.

Operation

Obviously, you need to know how to operate the spray, too. Is there a safety release? If so, how do you disengage it? Most pepper spray products available today allow for several bursts before the canister is empty. Keeping in mind your own safety as well as the safety of those who might be around you, go outside and fire the spray a couple of times. Keeping the safety on, practice the movements over and over, from removing the pepper spray from your pocket to pointing and shooting. Repeat this until it becomes muscle memory.

Cleanup

There are many proposed treatment protocols for decontaminating from accidental exposure to pepper spray. Anecdotal evidence suggests things like rinsing with clean water, washing with Dawn or similar dish soap, and even using baby shampoo might work. The reality is that the only sure method is time. Take off any clothes that were exposed, rinse off, then stay in open air for half an hour or so. Blink your eyes repeatedly so they tear, which will help rinse them. Cry and wait; it will get better soon.

ELECTROSHOCK WEAPONS

Electroshock weapons come in two basic types—stun guns and TASERs. Both work by using a high-voltage electrical current that temporarily paralyzes the target while also causing extreme pain. The electricity causes the muscles in the body to spasm uncontrollably. If you want to see and hear just how painful this can be, search YouTube for law enforcement training videos. As part of their training, officers are placed on the receiving end of electroshock weapons. The screams you'll hear are real.

Stun Guns

In the civilian world, stun guns are far more common than TASERs. Stun guns first started becoming available to the public in the mid-1980s and were rather popular right out of the gate. A stun gun, no matter how it is dressed up or camouflaged, has two metal prods sticking out from one end.

Stun gun

When you press the button or trigger, you'll see a cool arc of electricity suddenly come alive between those prods. That, along with the distinctive buzzing or crackling noise, may be enough to deter an attacker.

The downside to using a stun gun is it needs to make physical contact with the target. It is a close-range weapon. If you're close enough to touch an attacker with the stun gun, keep in mind that they are also close enough to grab you. The shock from the stun gun will not travel from them to you, so no worries there. But, they may wrap you up in their arms or otherwise grab you as they go down.

Stun guns work just fine through clothing, so there's no need for any attempted acrobatics in order to nail the assailant's neck or other bare skin. With a hit in the upper thigh, they're going to go down.

A quick Google search found stun guns disguised as cell phones, lipstick, flashlights, hairbrushes, and more. Fair warning, though. Don't for even a moment think you'll be able to sneak such weapons past security personnel at airports or in government buildings. They will know how to find them, and your journey will come to a rather rapid end.

TASERs

Here's a quick history lesson. "TASER" is actually an acronym. It stands for Thomas A. Swift's Electric Rifle. The

original weapon was invented in the early 1970s by a
NASA physicist named Jack Cover. As a child, he'd been
a fan of Tom Swift, the hero of many adventure novels
written for young people. One of those books was *Tom
Swift and His Electric Rifle*, in which Tom invents a rifle
that shoots electricity rather than bullets. Cover added the
middle initial "A" to Tom Swift's name, presumably to
make the acronym work a little better.

The TASER works by
firing two small metal
probes at the attacker.
These probes are con-
nected to the TASER
unit by means of thin
wires. The probes have

TASER

small hooks on the ends and are designed to penetrate
clothing and be difficult to remove. The user then acti-
vates the electric current, which travels through the wires
to the attacker. Firing the TASER is rather intuitive as it
is shaped like a handgun.

The original TASER units used gunpowder as the
propellant, which in turn meant it then fell under the
purview of the Bureau of Alcohol, Tobacco, Firearms, and
Explosives. Modern models use compressed gas instead
of gunpowder so they are no longer classified as firearms.

The probes are designed to go through clothing and reach the target's skin. However, the TASER is still effective even if the probes lodge in the clothing. As long as they are within close proximity to the skin's surface, the current will still flow. However, if one of the probes misses completely, the target won't receive the shock. Some TASER units are equipped with a stun gun feature that can be employed in those instances. Just as with the stun guns I talked about earlier, there are two metal studs that protrude from this type of unit. If those touch your target, the current will light them up.

TASERs are loaded with single-use cartridges. Once fired, you'll need to replace the cartridge before using the weapon again. This is in contrast to stun guns that utilize batteries and can be used repeatedly before battery replacement is necessary. Even the stun gun models that are rechargeable will allow the user several zaps before depleting the charge.

The average range of a TASER unit is about 15 feet. However, there does need to be a bit of a spread between the probes in order for the weapon to be most effective. As the probes fire from the weapon, they begin moving apart from each other. The weapon works best if the probes are 6 inches or more apart at the time of contact. This translates to a minimum distance from the target of about 4 or 5 feet when firing the TASER.

TASERs tend to be more expensive than stun guns, averaging a few hundred dollars or more. You should also research your local laws to ensure it is legal for you to carry and use a TASER. In some states, only certain types or models are allowed for civilian use.

Of the two main types of electroshock weapons, I tend to learn toward stun guns rather than TASERs. While they do require you to be closer to the assailant, stun guns allow for repeated uses without a reload.

FLASHLIGHTS

Few people realize just how disorienting a bright flashlight can be until they've experienced it themselves. I'm not talking about the cheap plastic flashlights you'll find at the hardware store, though. There are several truly powerful flashlights available today that make your daddy's Maglite seem like a birthday cake candle in comparison.

I alternate carrying one of two flashlights on a daily basis. The Streamlight ProTac 1AAA emits 70 lumens with the push of a button. I like this light because it is very bright, yet very small and slim. It easily slips into my pants

The Coast HX5 and the Streamlight ProTac 1AAA

pocket, and I can forget it is there until I need it. The other flashlight I carry is the Coast HX5. It is also a small but powerful light. Slightly larger than the ProTac 1AAA, the HX5 will throw 130 lumens, almost double the ProTac, using a standard alkaline battery.

Some of the larger flashlights, such as the Fenix TK15C, have a strobe setting that is specifically designed to distract and disorient an attacker. I would caution you, though, that if you suffer from epilepsy or any other condition that causes you to be rather vulnerable to strobes, do not go this route for a non-lethal option. It makes little sense to put yourself at risk for a seizure.

Most of the tactical flashlights sold today are metal and solid enough to be used as a blunt force weapon in a pinch. In fact, some flashlights even have crenulated heads designed to inflict damage against an attacker.

As for recommended size of the flashlight, that's going to depend on a few factors. First, if you plan on carrying the flashlight daily, you'll probably want something on the smaller side that will easily fit into a pocket or purse, such as the previously mentioned Streamlight ProTac 1AAA. Here's a good estimate for a minimum flashlight size: Grab a pencil and hold it in a clenched fist. Have the eraser end stick out from the bottom of your fist about half an inch. Make a mark on the other end of the pencil just where it exits your hand. Measure from the tip of the eraser to that mark. Look for a flashlight at least that long but that is also thin enough to hold comfortably in your fist.

Personally, I carry a flashlight because I frequently find the need for a portable source of light. In my day job as a private investigator, I'm constantly walking into dimly lit buildings. The possible self-defense uses are, for me, secondary to having the ability to see where I'm going and, hopefully, see who might be waiting for me. With that said, I don't overlook the possibility of using a flashlight to give me a quick advantage in an altercation. For that reason, I select flashlights that will do double duty for me.

LUMENS VS. WATTS

For many years, we shopped for light bulbs by searching for wattage ratings. For a kitchen ceiling light, you might want a 60-watt bulb. For a bedside lamp, a 40-watt bulb would usually suffice. When shopping for flashlights, instead of watts you'll find lumens as the measurement of power. The higher the number of lumens, the brighter the light.

A 40-watt bulb is roughly equivalent to 450 lumens. A 60-watt bulb is around 800 lumens. Bear in mind, though, that the light of an LED flashlight is far more concentrated than that of a bedside lamp. Even a mere 65 lumens is enough to dazzle an attacker when shined right into his eyes.

For defensive purposes, I'd recommend no less than 50 lumens.

The Streamlight ProTac 1AAA isn't a great choice for a weapon, but if jabbed into the face or solar plexus of an attacker, it should give me enough time to get away. Plus, even 70 lumens would be enough to dazzle someone's eyes for a bit.

RESTRAINTS

Restraints aren't weapons in a technical sense. But, given that they are not intended to be lethal, the discussion of restraints is suitable to this chapter. Restraints, as discussed here, include traditional handcuffs, the more modern nylon zip ties, and makeshift restraints, such as rope or other cordage.

My take on restraints is, unless you work in law enforcement, security, the military, or another related field,

Zip ties

there's no reason to carry them in your daily life. If you are attacked or otherwise end up in a confrontation, your primary goal is to get away, not to effect some sort of arrest or detention of the attacker.

Extending the discussion to include life after some sort of societal collapse, I'm still on the fence about using restraints. If you were to capture someone and restrain them, at some point you're going to have to take those restraints off. Depending on the overall situation, this could be just as dangerous, if not more so, than applying the restraints in the first place.

Applying restraints, especially to someone resisting you, is not an easy task. If you choose to carry restraints, seek out training from a qualified instructor and practice, practice, practice until you have it down pat. If you make one mistake out in the real world, you may find yourself cuffed and stuffed.

• • •

Non-lethal or less-than-lethal options are an important consideration in your overall security plan. In any confrontation, your ultimate goal is to get away from the attacker. A shot of pepper spray to the eyes or a zap from a stun gun to the neck will often suffice, giving you the opening you need to beat it and find help. Employing deadly force is not a decision to be made lightly and having non-lethal weapons at your disposal allows you some degree of latitude in how you handle a given situation.

CHAPTER 3
FIREARMS

Firearms are the best choice for just about any armed confrontation you can imagine. Whether it's for an attempted mugging in a back alley, a home invasion at 3:00 a.m., or repelling a group of post-collapse gang bangers looking to steal your food, if the weapon doesn't go boom, it will probably be less than ideal.

Firearms are intimidating, far more so than other weapons. An assailant, upon seeing you holding a handgun and witnessing the resolve in your eyes to use the weapon, will back off far more often than not. Firearms are also rather easy to use, at least compared to the arduous training necessary to wield a knife or baton effectively. At close range, especially, it becomes a matter of point and shoot.

WHY A FIREARM MIGHT NOT BE FOR YOU

Throughout this book, I repeatedly mention that a firearm is the weapon of choice in almost all situations. There are reasons, though, why someone may find it necessary to go armed with something other than a gun.

You are forbidden to possess a firearm. Perhaps you live in an area of the world where ownership of firearms by private citizens isn't allowed. Or, due to an indiscretion years ago, you are not able to legally possess a firearm. It could be that

THE COOPER COLOR CODE

Colonel Jeff Cooper is a legend in the firearms world. He was a United States Marine who served in both World War II and the Korean War. Colonel Cooper went on to found the American Pistol Institute in Arizona. He became a well-known instructor in handgun use.

One of the many things Colonel Cooper is remembered for is his development of the Cooper Color Code, which uses colors to indicate an individual's state of mind, level of awareness, and willingness to take action in combat. These levels are usually expressed as conditions, such as Condition White or Condition Red.

White: Completely and totally unprepared for anything. This person is easily surprised and basically clueless about the world around them. If they were attacked, they'd probably perish, unless the attacker was wildly inept or they were incredibly lucky.

firearm possession or ownership is allowed but you've not yet obtained the requisite permits or licenses. Whatever the case may be, I highly advise you to follow all applicable laws related to firearm ownership.

You have small children. Many parents choose to keep firearms out of the home while their children are young. While proper education and training coupled with common-sense precautions like safes and gun locks will greatly reduce the risk of accidents and such, the only guaranteed way to ensure no one is ever shot is to keep firearms out of the dwelling.

Yellow: Alert to possible threats but nothing specific is getting their attention. This person's eyes are roving, their head is on a swivel, and they are present in the world. They're noticing things, like the blue car that just turned the corner toward them, but they haven't cued in on any true threats.

Orange: A potential threat has caught this person's attention. They are focused on a specific target or situation and are ready to act if necessary. They mentally commit to a trigger point—if the potential offender does [blank], they will take action.

Red: Time for action. The situation has crossed the trigger point set during Condition Orange and this person is engaging according to their plan.

Many law enforcement trainers and military units have adopted or adapted the Cooper Color Code.

Your family members don't agree on firearm ownership. In any familial relationship, concessions must be made in order to keep the peace. For some, this means remembering to put the toilet seat down and replace the cap on the toothpaste. For others, firearms may be a sticking point. This isn't always a husband-and-wife issue, either. It could be you live with your parents or you have roommates, and they don't sit well with guns.

You can't afford a firearm. Unless you fall into the deal of a lifetime, firearms are an expensive proposition. Even at the low end of the spectrum, you can expect to pay a couple hundred dollars for a used handgun or rifle. Add to that the cost of ammunition, cleaning kits, and accessories, and firearms quickly rise out of the budgetary reach for many people.

FIREARM SELECTION

If you ask 10 different firearm aficionados for gun recommendations, you're likely to get 30 different answers. Everyone has their own favorites, from manufacturers to size, which is typically expressed as the caliber or, in the case of shotguns, the gauge. The caliber is the inside diameter of the firearm's barrel, as measured in hundredths of an inch. Not coincidentally, this is also the diameter of the bullet being fired. The barrel of a .45 caliber handgun has

TEACHING KIDS ABOUT FIREARMS

Education is important and can be a powerful tool against accidents. Teach your children from an early age that firearms are to be respected, not feared. As you feel they are ready for it, show them how to properly handle firearms. In many cases, accidental discharges have been the result of an untrained person not knowing how to properly handle the weapon. Show them and have them practice how to safely load and unload the weapon. Talk to them about what to do if they find a firearm, either in the home or out in the world. This could be as simple as leaving the firearm where it is and getting an adult. Having conversations like this will take the mystery out of firearms and give them the information they need to handle situations properly.

an inside diameter of 45/100 an inch. There's a lot involved when it comes to firearm selection including one's body size, hand size, strength, and comfort and familiarity with firearms in general.

The best way to select a firearm is to head to a gun shop and start handling different models. See what seems to fit your hands best and start there. Many gun ranges rent out firearms, which is a great way to test out different makes and models without having to plunk down hundreds of dollars on something you may later find just isn't suited for you.

Safety First

Before I get into the different types of firearms, I must stress the importance of safety. More so than any other weapon discussed in this book, firearms have the potential for sudden, catastrophic results in the event of improper use or handling. Once the trigger is pulled, there is absolutely no way to turn that bullet around.

Accidents happen. After all, we're only human. Even those individuals who have completed hundreds of hours of training and have fired thousands and thousands of rounds without incident can slip up. All it takes is a fraction of a second's inattention, a momentary lapse in focus.

Many different sets of rules have been developed in an effort to keep gun owners and users safe. Colonel Jeff Cooper, a world-renowned authority on handgun shooting, developed four such rules that cover just about everything. These rules apply no matter what type of firearm you're using, from a small handgun to a big-game hunting rifle.

1. Consider all guns as always loaded. Even if you personally cleared the weapon, treat it as though it is fully loaded and ready to fire.

2. Never let the muzzle face anything you are not willing to destroy. In other words, don't ever

point a firearm at something you do not want to shoot.

3. Keep your finger off the trigger until your sights are on the target. The only time you should touch the trigger is when you're about to fire the weapon. Otherwise, keep your finger outside of the trigger guard (see page 61).

4. Identify your target and what is behind it. Many firearms today are powerful enough that the round fired will go through the target and keep on going. Have absolutely no doubt about your target and where the bullet is going to go if it goes through the target completely.

Securing your firearms is also a key element to safety. Only those who are authorized to use the firearms should be able to access them. If the firearms aren't in use, they should be stored safely and responsibly.

The safest approach is to keep the firearms locked in a safe, with locks affixed to the triggers and the ammunition stored in a separate location. The presence of children in the home may call for increased security measures, such as multiple safes or locks on each firearm, whereas a single adult or even a family of grown-ups might not need such strict policies.

It may be difficult to respond with any degree of speed to a home invasion or other sudden event when your firearm is locked in a safe. The quicker you can get a loaded firearm into your hand during a crisis, the better. However, the safety of those who live in your home comes first. You'll need to find the balance point that works for you and your family. For some, that might mean keeping a loaded handgun in the home easily reached by you but (hopefully) inaccessible to your children. For example, you can buy a clock that has a hidden compartment for a handgun. Hang it on the wall near the front door so you will have a firearm in easy reach, just in case. For others, it might be reasonable to store a loaded firearm in each room of the home, hidden from view but ready to go at a moment's notice.

Securing your weapons against theft is important. Firearms are high-ticket items that are often sought by burglars. If you go to the trouble and expense of investing in a gun safe, use the darn thing. If you decide to squirrel away firearms throughout the house, know that if you can find them, so can someone else.

One more thing related to home security and firearms. You've no doubt seen signs and stickers on windows and doors that say things like, "This property is protected by Smith & Wesson." Or, "Trespassers will be shot. Survivors will be shot again." While some of these are clever and humorous, I don't recommend them as any sort of real deterrent to theft. All you are accomplishing is telling burglars that there may be firearms inside.

Think it through. Your Smith & Wesson security plan only works if someone is home. Bobby Burglar just waits for everyone to leave for work and school, then breaks in through a back window. Thanks to your ill-advised signage, he is not only searching for cash and portable electronics, he's on the hunt for the gun collection. Past experience has taught him to head for the master bedroom first. He starts with the nightstand drawers, then moves to the closet. In a matter of minutes, he's found two handguns, some sparkly jewelry, and the digital camera on the dresser. He'll probably remove and keep the SD card from the camera once he gets a look at the photos. You probably should have deleted them like you promised you would.

How much protection did your funny signs provide?

Affordability

A firearm, whether it's a handgun, rifle, or shotgun, is an investment. For one person, dropping a few hundred dollars on a pistol is like buying a loaf of bread at the grocery store. For another person, spending even a hundred dollars on an old and well-used .22 rifle requires at least a month or two of saving first. I'd bet most of my readers lean more toward the latter than the former.

If you see yourself making a firearm purchase in the future, I suggest you start saving money for it now. Even just a few dollars a week will add up over time. Keep an

BUYING A USED FIREARM

One of the best ways to stretch the firearms budget is to buy used rather than new. You can find some really good deals at gun shows, especially from people who are walking around with a gun in hand that they are looking to sell. Gun stores also usually have a selection of used weapons they've acquired.

Any time you buy something used, whether it is a firearm or a car, you run the risk of just buying someone else's problem. Therefore, it is important to know what to look for and thoroughly inspect the weapon before handing over your money. Until you have some experience under your belt, you might want to ask a knowledgeable friend or family member to accompany you.

- After receiving permission from the seller, pick up the firearm and ensure it is unloaded, then gently shake the weapon and listen. Any loose rattling is cause for concern.

- Ask about the history of the weapon. The seller may not know anything about the previous owner, but it never hurts to ask. If it seems obvious you're getting a story rather than any real information, that's a red flag that something isn't right with the deal. Most sellers are completely honest and forthcoming. Every once in a while, though, you'll run into a snake.

- Inspect the weapon on all sides. Minor nicks and scratches are normal and shouldn't affect the operation of the firearm.

eye out for used firearms for sale, both at gun shows as well as through newspaper ads and such. Cash is king and if you are able to show up with a handful of greenbacks,

However, if anything looks bent or if there is a missing screw or something, you may want to pass on the purchase.

- With the seller's permission, cycle the weapon a few times. This entails making sure all the parts that are supposed to move do so freely and the parts that aren't supposed to move stay put.

- If everything meets your expectations and you are going to make a reasonable offer on the weapon, ask if either you or the seller can field strip, or partially disassemble, the weapon so you can check the barrel and other interior parts. Don't take things this far unless you're ready to make the purchase, though, as it isn't fair to the seller to go through all that work just for giggles. If the bore (inside surface of the barrel) or other areas look dirty or rusty, that's a sign the weapon hasn't been properly maintained.

- Be fair when it comes to bargaining on a purchase. Haggling on the price of a used firearm is routine and expected, but be reasonable about it. Do your homework ahead of time so you know what the weapon is truly worth. Don't offer a ridiculously low price just to see if they'll bite. Odds are they won't and all you'll accomplish is irritating the seller. Take into account the condition of the weapon as well as any accessories the seller may include. More than once, I've paid a hair more than I wanted to for a firearm but made up for it by negotiating the inclusion of accessories like a holster or ammunition.

you're far more likely to be able to negotiate a lower price. Do your homework, too, and have at least a basic understanding of what different firearms are worth. If you lack the confidence in such matters, ask a friend or family member who has that knowledge to accompany you.

Prices for firearms fluctuate quite a bit based on geography as well as the relative popularity of a given make or model. Some brands, such as Glock, can command a higher price based on name recognition alone. In general, you can expect to pay around $200 for a shotgun or low-budget handgun. Add another $50 to $100 for a good-quality rifle. Those prices are for used weapons, too, not brand new.

Reliability

Once you've narrowed down your choices a bit, do some homework, online and otherwise, and research the manufacturers and models. If possible, stick with the names that have a long-standing reputation, such as Smith & Wesson and Ruger. There's a reason they are still in business after all these years. Glock is a relative newcomer, at least compared to Colt and Remington, but has an excellent reputation.

The thing is, you need for your firearm to go boom each and every time you pull the trigger. An inexpensive firearm from a no-name manufacturer is less likely to do that, due to design flaws or lesser quality components. After all, there's a reason the no-name brand is cheaper. Get the best you can afford and upgrade when possible.

Calibers

As you would expect, opinions from various experts differ as to the best caliber, or inside diameter of the barrel, for defense. The reality is, the decision should be a personal one, taking into account a few different factors. Note: With shotguns, the size of the barrel is referred to as the gauge, not the caliber. See page 72 for more information.

Comfort. This should be one of your first considerations. The size of the bullet is irrelevant if you're unable to accurately shoot it. The larger the bullet, the greater the recoil. Physics plays a role in firearm and caliber selection. Remember, for every action, there is an equal and opposite reaction. Keeping the math out of the equation, this means that the larger the caliber, the more force it has upon impact, but the more recoil you'll feel when the bullet is fired. That said, the size of the handgun comes into play, too. As I mentioned earlier, a smaller pistol is going to absorb less recoil than a full-size model. Most handguns are available in at least a few different calibers. What I suggest is choosing the handgun that fits your hand best, then looking for a model chambered in the largest caliber you're able to shoot comfortably. This takes—you guessed it—practice and experimentation to determine.

Expense. I've mentioned practicing and trying out different handguns several times already. This brings up the next consideration, expense. Ammunition is expensive and will only become more so as time goes on. Gone are the days when heading to the range to burn through a few boxes of ammo could be done on a whim. Today, it seems like you'd almost need a second mortgage on the house in order to afford a serious amount of range time. Compare the prices of the calibers you're considering and realize you might have to compromise on a slightly smaller caliber in order to better afford the practice you probably need to reach and maintain an acceptable level of proficiency. Marksmanship is a skill that will deteriorate over time without practice.

Stopping power. A low-caliber weapon, such as a .22 Long Rifle, or .22 LR, is lethal, no question, but unless you hit something vital, you aren't likely to stop your assailant right in his tracks. As I said before, choose the largest caliber you can comfortably shoot. Many experts say that the .380 or .38 Special calibers would be the absolute smallest ones you should consider for defensive purposes. The .380 caliber has become quite popular in recent years. Many manufacturers offer small-size handguns chambered for that round, marketing them specifically for concealed carry.

The 9 mm round is very common and is in use today by numerous law enforcement agencies as well as our military. It works, no question about it, and has a little less recoil that some of the alternatives.

Ruger LCP

Handguns chambered in .357 Magnum have a bonus in that they will also fire .38 Special rounds (though the reverse is not true), giving you more bang for your buck in a rather literal sense. What this means in a practical sense is those in the home who would feel more comfortable shooting a smaller caliber will be able to practice and use the same handgun as someone else who is fine shooting the higher powered .357 Mag round.

The .40 S&W cartridge has plenty of stopping power. It is a favorite of law enforcement officers for that reason. I know several law enforcement officers and they are pretty evenly split between the 9 mm and .40 S&W.

If it feels comfortable and you can swing it financially, the .45 ACP, will certainly do the job. It is a large bullet, sometimes referred to as a slow-moving bullet, that packs a wallop when it hits. Keep in mind that that's relative to other calibers. It isn't like the bullet is a slow freight train and someone can just casually step out of the way.

Commonality. Commonality is another factor to keep in mind. If you select a firearm that uses an obscure caliber, you might find it all but impossible to locate ammunition when times get harsh. Even in good times, you might have to pay through the nose.

Standardization. If you plan to acquire several firearms, it might make things easier in the long run if most or all of them fire the same size bullet. The fewer the number of calibers you need to keep on hand, the better for both practicality of use and affordability.

Maintenance

A firearm should be cleaned after each use. The cleaning and maintenance routine will be slightly different for each firearm. If your weapon didn't come with an owner's manual, find one online. The manual will give you the exact instructions on how to field strip your firearm for cleaning.

I like to thoroughly clean and oil any firearm that has been sitting for several months. This ensures it is always in good condition and ready to fire if necessary.

The first few times you clean a firearm, it is very helpful to have someone with you who is experienced in the process. They will be able to point out things you may miss as well as show you tips and tricks they may have picked up over time.

The supplies necessary for cleaning a firearm are listed below.

Note: Bore brushes come in different sizes. Make sure you get the proper one for your firearm. The brush packages are always labeled with the applicable firearm(s) for the brush. Be sure to pick up at least one extra bore brush for each caliber of firearm you own. The brushes do wear down over time.

You'll also go through a small stack of patches each time you clean a firearm. Buy a few packages of them to make sure you always have enough on hand.

There are numerous kits available that contain most of these items or you can purchase them individually as needed.

- Towel or plastic garbage bag

- Gun vise, two small sandbags, or gun cleaning pad

- Bore brush

- Cleaning rod

- Solvent

- Patches and patch holder

- Small flashlight or bore light

- Old toothbrush

- Rags

- Gun oil

- Cotton swabs

Step 1. Prepare the area. Lay down a towel or a plastic garbage bag to protect the table or counter. The area should be well ventilated. Gather all of your cleaning supplies and place them nearby for convenience. (For long guns like rifles, you will want to invest in a gun vise or at least a couple of small sandbags to keep the weapon stationary as you work. A soft gun cleaning pad works well for handguns.)

Step 2. Unload the firearm, then field strip it according to the owner's manual. Keep all parts together so nothing gets lost.

Step 3. Attach the bore brush to the cleaning rod. Put solvent on the brush and work the brush through the barrel several times to loosen any debris and material in the barrel.

Step 4. Remove the brush from the cleaning rod and attach the patch holder. Work the patches through the barrel one at a time until the patches come through clean. The first few will be very soiled. Always run the patches through in one direction, from the breech (rear portion of the barrel) to the muzzle (where the projectile exits) or back to front. When the patch comes through on the front end of the barrel, remove it from the rod and pull the rod back through before attaching a new patch.

Step 5. Use a flashlight or bore light to look through the barrel and see if there is still any debris stuck to the interior. If there is, repeat the steps with the bore brush and patches.

Step 6. Once the barrel is clean, put some gun oil on a patch and run it through the barrel. This small coating of oil will protect the inside of the barrel from moisture.

Step 7. For revolvers, you'll also need to perform all of those steps for each of the chambers in the cylinder. The chambers are where the bullets are held in the cylinder.

Step 8. Next, clean the outside of the firearm. Use an old toothbrush and a bit of solvent to clean any dirt and grease from the various parts of the firearm. Use cotton swabs to get into all of the nooks and crannies. Use a rag to wipe everything down after you've scrubbed the parts.

Step 9. Apply lubricant to the appropriate points of the firearm. These points will vary from gun to gun, which is one more reason why it is important to have the appropriate owner's manual with you as you learn the cleaning process. No matter what, though, less is more when it comes to gun oil. Just a drop or two in each location will suffice.

Step 10. Reassemble the firearm and work the moving parts back and forth a bit to help spread the lubricant properly. Wipe down the entire weapon with a clean rag. A light coating of oil on the exposed surfaces will help preserve the finish. I've found that there is usually just enough lubricant seeping from the various joints of the firearm that wiping it all down with a rag spreads the extra oil perfectly. If that's not the case for you, apply just a few drops of oil to a rag and wipe down the weapon.

BASIC FIREARM TYPES
Handguns

Judged strictly on self-defense features, handguns top my list of firearms. Rifles and shotguns, which I'll discuss shortly, are more powerful but are difficult to carry or conceal as you go about your daily life. Handguns, however, are easy to strap on to a belt, and once you get used to the weight, you'll almost forget it is there until or unless you need it.

Handguns come in two basic types: revolvers and semi-automatics. Each has its own pros and cons, as summarized below.

Revolvers

I often refer to revolvers as cowboy guns because that seems to be a good point of reference for people who aren't familiar with firearms. Revolvers carry the ammunition in a rotating cylinder that most commonly contains six rounds. As the hammer is pulled back, the cylinder moves a bullet into firing position. When the trigger is pulled, the hammer falls and fires the bullet.

Revolvers come in three models: single action, double action, and double action only, all of which refer to the way the handgun is cocked.

Smith and Wesson Model 36 snubnose revolver

Single-action revolver. With a single-action revolver, the hammer must be pulled back manually before each shot. If you recall seeing any old Western movies where a character would slap the back of his handgun as he shot multiple rounds, that was a single-action revolver in use.

Double-action revolver. A double-action revolver allows the user to cock and fire the handgun with a single long pull of the trigger. As the trigger is pulled, the hammer cocks back and is then released. However, a double-action revolver will also allow the user to cock the hammer manually, just like the single-action ones. Doing so shortens the distance the trigger travels before the hammer falls. It also serves to lessen the amount of force needed to pull the trigger. Many shooters will manually cock a double-action revolver for the first shot, then rely upon the long trigger pull for subsequent shots.

Double-action-only revolver. The double-action-only revolver does not allow for manual cocking of the hammer. In fact, in most cases, the user can't even access the hammer as it is shrouded by the handgun's frame. This type of revolver was designed with concealment and rapid deployment in mind. When a revolver is deep inside a pocket or hidden in some other location on your person, the hammer could get caught on clothing as it is pulled out. The double-action-only models solve that problem by concealing the hammer completely. The trade-off, though, is you lack the ability to cock the weapon manually and each shot will necessitate the long trigger pull. A longer trigger pull can negatively affect your aim until you've practiced enough to compensate for it.

Loading and unloading. Most revolvers in production today utilize a swing-out cylinder for loading and unloading. On these models, the cylinder release is a button that is typically located on the left side of the weapon, just behind the cylinder. The button is pushed and the cylinder swings out to the left. An ejector pin is located on the front of the cylinder, right in the center. Pushing it will cause all rounds in the cylinder to pop up a bit for easy removal. New bullets are then loaded into the cylinder.

I recommend using a speed loader. This device allows you to load all of the bullets into the cylinder at once, rather than having to do it one at a time. These cylindrical tools are

Open cylinder, ready for loading

loaded with bullets at home, then carried in a pocket or perhaps a pouch on your belt. When needed, you dump the spent rounds from the revolver, then insert new ones into the cylinder with the speed loader. The speed loader will either have a button or a rotating knob on the back that releases the bullets into the cylinder. Speed loaders are firearm-specific, meaning you'll need to shop around to find one made for your particular firearm.

Revolvers are, by and large, rather uncomplicated as far as weapons go. Don't get me wrong, the parts are all machined to exacting standards. But they tend to be very reliable and jam free. There just aren't that many moving parts to get fouled up.

The downside is the relatively small number of bullets it can fire before needing a reload. While it largely depends on the caliber, most revolvers carry six shots. If you're up against a single intruder, that may be plenty. However, to paraphrase my old buddy Bill Shakespeare, if your sorrows come not as single spies but as battalions, the more firepower you can bring to the party, the better. Your accuracy will be negatively affected by low light conditions, adrenaline, and other factors that are likely to be present in a defensive encounter. As a result, you may decide that the more ammunition you can carry in the weapon, the better.

Semi-Automatics

Semi-autos are a bit more complicated than revolvers. When the trigger is pulled on a semi-automatic handgun, a lot of things happen in rapid succession. First, the hammer falls and fires the bullet through the bar-

Glock 30

rel and, hopefully, toward your intended target. Next, the slide on the top of the weapon slams backward, which cocks the hammer for the next shot. The spent round is ejected and a new round is stripped from the magazine and loaded into firing position. All of this happens almost instantaneously.

Let's run through a little terminology, so you might better understand the above.

Magazine. Where semi-autos carry ammunition, most commonly inserted into the handle of the handgun. The magazine will either be a single or double stack.

- **Single-stack magazine:** Keeps all rounds stacked evenly on top of one another in a single column.

- **Double-stack magazine:** Keeps all rounds staggered slightly to each side as the

Single-stack magazine

  column rises, allowing for double the capacity of the single-stack magazines. The double-stack magazine is usually a bit thicker to compensate for the staggered rounds.

Clip. The slang term for magazine, which is like fingernails on a chalkboard to many firearm instructors.

Hammer. This part of the firearm resembles a small lever that snaps forward when the trigger is pulled. The hammer hits the firing pin, which in turn fires the bullet.

Trigger guard. A band of metal or plastic that surrounds the trigger, preventing a finger from accidentally firing the weapon.

Slide. This part of the handgun runs along the top of the weapon and slides back and forth. The slide is used to cock the weapon and chamber a round.

Semi-auto handgun with slide pulled back

Most semi-autos are double action, which means the same as it does with revolvers. The hammer can be pulled back manually, or it can be pulled back and fired with a long trigger pull. However, that only applies to the first shot. As noted at the beginning of this section, when the semi-auto is fired, the slide moves back and cocks the hammer for the next round. This makes for a slightly more rapid-fire weapon than the revolver because after that first shot is fired, the trigger's travel distance is shorter and the pull is lighter.

The magazine capacity is one of the true pluses of the semi-auto handgun. Where a revolver carries an average of six bullets, the full-size semi-auto, depending upon the model, could carry 12 or more. Note, however, that some states and municipalities have enacted bans against what are termed high-capacity magazines, which are generally understood to be magazines that carry 10 or more rounds.

Notice that I specified the "full-size" semi-auto above. The smaller the semi-auto, the fewer rounds it will carry, which stands to reason. There are some very compact semi-auto handguns on the market, such as those in the .380 caliber, marketed specifically for concealed carry. Some people refer to them as "pocket pistols." A drawback with these compact models is there is less gun to absorb recoil when it is fired. Granted, the caliber is fairly small, too, so it isn't like you're going to have to pick yourself up off the ground after firing it. But, in some cases, there's enough recoil to get your attention. Yet one more reason why it is important to test out different firearms before purchasing one.

Semi-auto handguns are typically flatter than revolvers, which makes them a bit easier to conceal for daily carry. However, they do have more moving parts and can be subject to jamming and other issues, especially if not cleaned and maintained properly.

Rifles

The basic definition for a rifle is a shoulder-fired weapon with a barrel that contains grooves, called "rifling," that impart a spin on the bullet as it leaves the weapon. This spin stabilizes the bullet in flight, allowing for a high degree of accuracy.

Rifles come in many shapes and sizes. I've grouped them into four categories: bolt action, lever action, carbine, and assault rifle.

Bolt action. If you've seen what most people refer to as a deer rifle, you've seen a bolt-action rifle. The bolt action is, by far, the most common type of rifle used for hunting. It is likely the most reliable type of rifle used today, and it is extremely accurate. Military snipers used bolt actions for these reasons, as do hunters. If the situation requires a precision shot rather than just sending as much lead downrange as possible, the bolt action is the way to go.

Bolt-action rifle

At the top of the bolt-action rifle, typically on the right side, is a small handle. This handle operates the bolt, which slides open the breech (the rear section of the barrel). Upon opening, the spent cartridge, if there is one, is removed. A fresh round is then inserted into the breech and the bolt is closed, making the rifle ready to fire again. With some practice, this entire process only takes a second.

A good-quality riflescope is considered a requisite piece of equipment. Leupold Optics make among the best you can buy in that regard. A bolt-action rifle is a long-distance weapon. It isn't, or shouldn't be, your go-to weapon for in-home defense situations. Rather, this is what you want on hand for those occasions when you need to reach out and touch someone a few football fields away.

Because the bolt is operated manually, none of the energy or gas from the firing bullet is siphoned off to eject a spent shell and/or cycle a new round. This means the bolt-action rifle is capable of firing higher powered rounds than other types of rifles. The bolt action is also extremely reliable. It has only a few moving parts so there isn't much there to get messed up in foul weather or other bad conditions.

One more great feature of the bolt-action rifle is that if you're lying down in a hidden position, you won't need to roll yourself or the weapon to the side to chamber a new round. However, you will need to remove your hand from the trigger guard to operate the bolt, which can result in having to re-aim each shot.

The .308 cartridge is a great, all around cartridge for a bolt-action rifle. It will serve well for hunting medium and large game as well as for hitting targets at a distance. Another round that is great for these purposes is the 30.06 cartridge.

Lever action. With the lever-action rifle, the movement to cycle a round takes place at the bottom of the rifle rather than the top, as is the case with the bolt action. Just behind the trigger is a lever, often attached to the trigger guard.

Pulling the lever down ejects the spent cartridge. Pushing the lever back into position causes a new round to be chambered. Unlike the bolt-action rifle, the lever action also has an exposed hammer that must be cocked manually prior to firing.

Lever-action rifle

Where the bolt action has a box magazine, the lever action's magazine is tubular and positioned directly under the barrel in most cases. Depending on the make, model, and caliber, expect the capacity to be around 6 to 10 rounds. While not great for a sustained firefight, that should be plenty for most defensive encounters.

Earlier in this chapter, I mentioned the possibility of standardizing your firearms so you only need to stock one caliber. The lever-action rifle can be a great option in that regard. Pick up one chambered for a .357 Magnum and get the handguns to match.

An advantage the lever action has over the bolt action is length. Lever-action rifles are generally shorter than their bolt-action counterparts, which makes them better suited for indoor use. Most lever-action rifles come equipped with open sights, and these are usually sufficient for the majority of situations.

The lever action is equally suitable to both left-handed and right-handed individuals. Either hand can operate the lever without a problem. With standard bolt-action rifles, the bolt handle is on the right side, which can cause difficulty for left-handed shooters. Lever actions also tend to be faster to operate than bolt-action rifles.

There are a few drawbacks to the lever action. If you're shooting from a prone position, you'll need to rotate the rifle about 90 degrees to be able to cycle a new round, due to the location of the lever. This amount of movement could expose you to detection from someone trying to find your position.

Also, the lever-action rifle isn't suited for extremely high-powered calibers. That's not a deal breaker, of course, but something to consider if you're only planning to purchase a single rifle and are debating between bolt-action and lever-action models.

Personally, I like lever-action rifles quite a bit. I think they are a valuable part of a prepper's arsenal, especially when you consider the standardization of ammunition capability.

Carbine. Technically, a carbine is just a rifle with a short barrel. It used to be that a carbine was a smaller version of an existing rifle, sort of like the difference between a full-size semi-auto handgun and a compact handgun. It fires the same rounds, just from a smaller and lighter package. Over the years, though, manufacturers started coming out with smaller-size rifles that had no larger companion pieces and just calling them carbines right from the beginning.

Bushmaster M4A3 carbine

To complicate matters further, it has become understood that any rifle that fires a pistol caliber is also termed a carbine, regardless of barrel length. Granted, you aren't going to find many large, long rifles shooting pistol calibers, so they'd probably be termed carbines by default anyway.

The advantage of a carbine is in the smaller size. The shorter barrel makes it easier to maneuver through the home or in urban environments. It is also generally a lighter weapon than other rifles, which is a definite plus if you'll be carrying it for any length of time.

One of the most popular carbines today is the Ruger Mini-14. It shoots the .223 Remington cartridge, which is one of the most common calibers found in the United States. Where the Ruger Mini-14 particularly shines is with aftermarket accessories. It is sort of like the Tinkertoy sets you may have played with as a child. You can quite literally change your Ruger Mini-14's appearance from a hunting rifle to an assault rifle very easily.

Assault rifle. These are the dreaded "black guns" you may have heard referenced in the news. They can be quite intimidating, that's for sure. And that's not a bad thing, either, provided you're on the trigger end of the weapon.

AR-15

Among the most common are the AR platform weapons. The AR stands for Armalite, which is the company that originated the design back in the 1950s. There have been so many manufacturers making similar weapons over the years that, like Kleenex and Spandex, the brand name has become the common name.

The AR rifles are reliable, fire a common (.223 Remington) round, and have a ton of aftermarket accessories available. For many preppers and survivalists, the AR rifle tops the list of defense firearms.

AK-47

Another weapon worth considering is the AK-47 or one of its variants. These are the most widely used assault rifles on the planet. Simply put, they'll last darn near forever with even minimal care and maintenance. They are robust weapons capable of taking a beating and coming back looking for more. They fire a 7.62x39 mm round, which will put large holes in whatever it hits. The magazines used with the AK-47 are immediately recognizable due to their curved shape.

Submachine Guns

The submachine gun sort of bridges the gap between pistol and carbine. While they are in regular use by law enforcement and some military units, the weapons

Uzi submachine gun

typically lack the power to penetrate body armor and therefore have often been sidelined in favor of assault rifles.

If you were a fan of action movies in the 1980s, you no doubt saw numerous instances of Uzi submachine guns in use. This Israeli firearm has become one of the most common submachine guns ever. Another well-known submachine gun is the Heckler & Koch MP5, which is very popular with law enforcement agencies in particular.

Submachine guns have what I'd consider a limited role in the survivalist arsenal. The extended magazine capacity allows you to fill the air with lead if the circumstances warrant doing so. But, by the same token, these weapons aren't cheap. I would recommend them only after meeting your other firearm needs first.

Shotguns

Next on the list of defensive firearms is the venerable shotgun. The sound of a shell being racked is very intimidating, let alone the roar that is let loose upon pulling the trigger. Shotguns most commonly fire two basic types of shells: shot shells and slugs.

Shot shells are filled with small pellets of varying size and quantity. This is denoted by numbers and sometimes letters, with the size of the pellets being inversely proportional to the numeric or alphabetical designation. For example, No. 8 shot consists of pellets far smaller than the ones in a No. 3 shell. Because they are smaller, a larger number of them will fit into the shell.

Slugs, on the other hand, consist of a single large pellet in the shell. If you decide to use slugs, invest in a rifled barrel for your shotgun. This is a special barrel that is grooved on the inside. These grooves, called rifling, increase the stability of the slug or bullet when it leaves the barrel. While you can shoot slugs through the standard barrel, your accuracy might suffer. In general, I don't advise using slugs for defense because doing so negates the advantages of a shotgun in an armed encounter. A shotgun is not a precision instrument, but therein lies its beauty. When loaded with shot shells, the shotgun allows for a little leeway when it comes to accuracy. As the pellets leave the barrel, they begin to spread. This means you don't need pinpoint marksmanship to do some damage. As the pellets strike the target, they do so somewhat at an angle while spreading, creating numerous wound channels in the target's body.

Gauge

Unlike handguns, rifles, and submachine guns, shotguns come in gauges rather than calibers. The gauge is a unit of measurement defining the size of the shotgun's barrel. The mathematical formula for determining the gauge of a firearm makes my head hurt. Suffice it to say, there are a few different shotgun gauges readily found on the market today.

- The 12-gauge shotgun is by far the most common. The Remington 870 12-gauge shotgun is perhaps the single most popular shotgun in the country when it comes to law enforcement or home defense. There are many variants, including the 870 Express and the 870 Wingmaster. For home defense, any of them will suffice.

- The 20-gauge shotgun is often used by bird hunters. It has a little less power and less recoil than the 12-gauge. The .410 is also fairly popular. More and more often, though, I've seen people using the .410 shot shells in combination guns like the Taurus Judge, which fires both .410 shells and .45 Colt cartridges. Some people swear by this weapon in particular, especially for use as a snake gun.

Remington 870 shotgun with pistol grip

Action

For the purposes of this discussion, there are two primary types of shotguns: pump action and break action. The pump-action shotgun has a sliding mechanism on the fore end that discharges the spent shell and loads a new one from the magazine. After firing a shell, the shooter pulls back on the pump. This causes the spent shell to exit the firearm and a new shell to be put into loading position. The pump is then pushed forward, loading the shell into firing position.

The break-action shotgun is a far older style. Double-barreled shotguns are among the most common styles used today that utilize the break action. With this model, the shotgun is hinged. A latch keeps everything in place. When loading or unloading, the latch is released and the barrels of the shotgun fold forward. Two shells are placed into the breech, which is the

Break-action shotgun

rear portion of the barrels. The shotgun is then folded back together and is ready to fire. This is obviously a slower process than that of the pump-action shotgun. But break-action shotguns are almost foolproof in that there are very few moving parts.

There are other, less common styles of shotguns, including lever action and bolt action. By and large, though, the pump action is the most common for home defense. Personally, I've always wanted a sawed-off double-barrel shotgun, à la Mad Max. Highly illegal, of course, and not very practical, but high on the points scale for coolness.

Ammunition

As noted earlier, shotguns fire shells rather than bullets. Shot shells are preferred over slugs when it comes to defense. Buckshot is far and away the most common type of shell used for this purpose by law enforcement, the military, and private citizens. Buckshot differs from bird shot in that the pellets are larger as well as fewer in number in each shell.

That said, bird shot is actually a great option for defense within the home. Using it will help avoid overpenetration, which is a serious consideration. Overpenetration occurs when the bullet or shot pellets go through a wall, possibly hitting a family member or even someone in the next house. Bird shot will do quite a bit of damage at close range but isn't likely to go through a standard wall and into the next room.

There exists a range of specialty ammunition for shotguns, too, though the cost of them may by prohibitive for the average homeowner. Flechette shells contain 20 or so small darts rather than shot pellets. They work well at penetrating some types of body armor. They are pretty expensive, though, running at around $20 for three shells.

Shells that use rubber pellets are available for a non-lethal option, commonly used by law enforcement agencies for riot control. Similar to this are the bean bag shells, which fire, well, bean bags filled with lead shot.

If you shop around, you can find shells that contain both buckshot and bird shot, which could be interesting. I've seen hollow slug shells designed to use some sort of combustible material, allegedly turning the slug into a small bomb that detonates upon impact. I haven't used them myself, so can't vouch for their reliability, but can say they sound extremely dangerous to use.

Then we have Dragon's Breath shells. These shells are loaded with magnesium, which ignites upon firing the shell. This produces a stream of fire about 100 feet long. Imagine a very short-lived flamethrower, and you have it about right. Obviously, using this indoors would be a very bad idea. Even using it outdoors might be questionable. But if you absolutely, positively must set someone on fire at fairly close range, this might be the way to go.

THE RECOMMENDED PREPPER FIREARM ARSENAL

Okay, here's the deal. Every single one of you reading this book will have slightly, or not so slightly, different firearm needs. On top of that are budget, firearm familiarity, and legal constraints. There is no possible way I could come up with a recommended arsenal that will fit every reader.

Instead, here is the order I recommend you acquire firearms. As your needs and budget allow, work your way down the list. Feel free to skip categories of weapons if you feel they are unnecessary or if, perhaps, they are prohibited by law in your area.

One more caveat I need to address. Even though the focus here is on defense, as preppers and survivalists, we need to always consider other uses for anything we purchase. With firearms, you may need to hunt food far more often than you need to fire on another human being. With that in mind, here we go.

1. **22 Rifle.** The .22 rifle is perhaps the most useful firearm you can purchase. With it, you can fill your cooking pot with anything from squirrel to big game, as well as defend your home. Plus, even at today's inflated prices, the ammunition isn't so expensive so as to be prohibitive. While it wouldn't be my first choice to use in a gun battle, it would do the job until I could get to something larger.

2. **Handgun.** If we were strictly looking at home defense situations, the handgun would be a bit further down the list. However, if you're out

and about, you won't be able to carry a carbine or shotgun everywhere you go. The handgun is the best choice for concealed carry. It is a great option for home defense, too.

3. **Shotgun.** There is perhaps no sound more pants filling to an intruder than that of a shell being racked in a shotgun. It is a universal sound, one that isn't easily mistaken for anything else on the planet. A shotgun offers low risk of overpenetration in a home defense situation. Loaded with buckshot, it can be used to take down big game. Bird shot will handle the smaller stuff.

4. **Carbine.** Again, thinking of home defense, the shorter barrel weapons work best. The carbine is also an excellent choice for close-range hunting. Shooter's choice as to whether they want something more traditional, like the lever-action carbines that fire pistol calibers, or something more militaristic in appearance. Both work equally well.

5. **Rifle.** A 30.06 deer rifle isn't the best choice for most home defense scenarios, if only because you probably don't want to shoot both the intruder in the living room as well as your neighbor in the next house over. But, for hunting large game, this

is the best option. Who knows what the future holds? Could be that the large game you end up hunting walks on two legs and is stalking your home from afar.

• • •

From this point, look further at your situation and what you may need for additional armaments. Keep in mind that you'll need plenty of ammunition for practice as well as real-world use. I feel it is better to have fewer firearms but with abundant ammunition rather than a whole lot of boom sticks without a lot of bullets.

CHAPTER 4
PROJECTILE WEAPONS

Simply put, the weapons in this chapter will put holes in a target but don't use gunpowder to do so. On the upside, this means they are quieter than firearms and the ammunition is usually cheaper than bullets. In fact, several of the weapons discussed use ammunition you could easily make or scrounge on your own.

The downside is they are nowhere near as powerful as firearms, and several of them would be difficult to use effectively indoors. There are far more effective weapons than a bow and arrow to use when confronting an intruder in the living room at three in the morning.

That said, these weapons all share a few excellent features. They are generally silent, which could be important in many scenarios, especially in a time when law and order are not being recognized. If you are averse to firearms, the options I'm going to present in this chapter may be your best bet for some sort of ranged weapon.

BOW AND ARROW

When I was a young boy, I made a bow from a curved stick and a bungee cord. I crafted arrows from some thin reeds, sharpening the tips and carving notches on the other end of each with my pocket knife. Believe it or not, the bow actually worked fairly well. I mean, I doubt I could have successfully hunted any-thing with it, but at eight years old, I thought it was pretty darn cool.

Longbow

It wasn't until a few years later that I learned it wasn't the string that provided the power on a real bow, but the stave, or the actual bow part of the contraption. As the string is pulled back, the stave is flexed. When the arrow is released, the stave is able to release that pressure forcefully, thrusting the arrow through the air.

Recent popular movies and television shows aside, the bow isn't really a high-speed weapon. It takes time to grab an arrow from the quiver, place the arrow on the string (this is called nocking), pull back the string, line up the target, and release the arrow. Few people in real life can toss five or six tennis balls into the air then nail each of them with an arrow in a matter of a couple of seconds.

Bows come in three basic types: longbow, recurve, and compound. Longbows are the simplest as well as the largest. A longbow stave, usually about as tall as the archer, is bent slightly and then a string is run between the ends. Because of the size of the bow, this is a weapon entirely unsuited for any sort of realistic indoor defense situation. However, if one needs a weapon with some decent range, this might be the way to go. With practice and the right equipment, 200 yards is a feasible distance for a longbow's range.

Recurve bow

Recurve bows are similar to longbows, but the stave sort of curls a bit at each end. Recurve bows are much more powerful than longbows and have the bonus of being a bit easier to shoot. Because of the way the bow is shaped, there is a lot of power being harnessed when the arrow is pulled back on the string. At the same time, the shape makes it easier to hold the bow in place while aiming as the archer isn't, or shouldn't be, struggling against the pull weight of the string.

The compound bow is what happened when technology started getting involved with archery. By placing pulleys at each end of the stave, archers were able to really ramp up the power without sacrificing accuracy. With recurve bows and longbows, the more powerful the bow, the harder it is to pull back and hold the string for any length of time. The compound bow largely eliminates that issue. As a compound bow's string is pulled

Compound bow

back, a point is reached where the force needed to hold the string back is greatly reduced. This is due to the shape and design of the pulley system of the bow. This allows the archer to hold the arrow on target for long periods of time without fatigue.

Of the three styles, the compound bow would be the most difficult to manufacture out of scavenged or scrounged materials. It is also the most difficult to maintain due to the many moving parts and different components at work.

If you are serious about investing in a bow, do yourself a favor and visit a pro shop to be fitted. Yes, just like having a suit custom made, there are all sorts of measurements that should be taken into account when buying a bow. I'm not saying you need to buy a custom bow right off the bat. But knowing those measurements will allow you to shop for a bow that is best suited to you.

Anatomy of a Bow

When shopping for a bow, it is helpful to have an understanding of some basic terminology.

Upper limb. The part of the bow that runs from the riser upward.

Lower limb. The part of the bow that runs from the riser downward.

String nock. Where the bow string is attached on the upper and lower limbs of longbows or recurve bows.

Idler wheel. The pulley at the end of the upper limb on a compound bow.

Cam. The pulley at the end of the lower limb on a compound bow.

Bow string. The cordage that attaches the upper and lower limbs.

Riser. The part of the bow that runs between the upper and lower limbs. This is also where you'll find the grip.

Grip. The part of the bow you hold as you pull back the bowstring.

Arrow rest. The upper surface of the grip where the arrow rests until fired. This is sometimes a separate piece attached to the bow.

Nock point. The spot on the bow string where the arrow is nocked or fitted until fired.

Bow Measurements

Draw length is the first and most important measurement. It is the distance from the grip to the nock point, plus 1¾ inches. You can find this measurement yourself with help from a friend. Stand up straight and extend your arms out to each side with your palms facing outward. Have your friend measure the distance in inches from the tip of one middle finger to the tip of the opposite middle finger. Take that number and divide it by 2.5. This will give you your proper draw length. However, bear in mind that not all bodies are created equal. If you have relatively short or long arms for your body size, that will affect your draw length. That's why I suggest visiting a pro shop to be fitted by an expert. Incidentally, the draw length also tells you the arrow size you should be using.

Draw length is particularly important when shopping for compound bows. Because of the way compound bows

CHOOSING THE PROPPER ARROW FOR YOUR BOW

The best way to determine the proper size and weight of the arrow you need is to take your bow with you to the store and ask a knowledgeable salesperson to assist you.

An arrow isn't a complicated piece of machinery, but there are a few terms you'll want to know when shopping.

Point: The sharp end that goes into the target.

Shaft: The straight section of the arrow running from the point to the nock.

Fletching: The plastic or feather pieces at the back end of the arrow. These stabilize the arrow as it flies.

Index vane: Often, of the three fletches on a typical arrow, one will be a different color from the other two. This index vane is a visual cue on how to position the arrow when nocking it. Keep the index vane pointed outward from the bow.

Nock: The slotted end of the arrow that fits onto the bow string.

There are actually a lot of factors that come into play with arrow selection. Here are just a couple of highlights.

Earlier, I talked about determining your draw length. You need this measurement when shopping for arrows as well as bows. Add 1 or 2 inches to your draw length and that's the arrow length you need. The average arrow length seems to fall around 29 or 30 inches.

As should be obvious, you want your arrows to be as straight as possible. Inspect every arrow individually to ensure consistent straightness. After shooting arrows, either for target practice or when hunting, check the arrows again before storing them to make sure none have suffered any damage. If they do get bent, set them aside and purchase replacements.

Another factor is arrow weight. Arrow weight is measured in grains per inch (gpi). A lighter arrow is fast and flies flatter but lacks the kinetic power of a heavier arrow. Hunters choose arrow weight based upon their intended prey. For example, for animals up to and including deer, an arrow of 7 to 9 gpi will suffice. For larger animals, like elk or moose, go heavier with 9 gpi or more. A human being is closer to a deer than a moose in size. That said, a heavier arrow is a little more forgiving when it comes to accuracy. Furthermore, it isn't like people are going to be dodging out of the way of a slow, heavier arrow as opposed to a fast, light one.

An arrow's "spine" refers to its stiffness. There are a few factors that determine the arrow's spine, such as the length of the shaft, the weight of the tip, and the material used to make the arrow. An arrow needs to have some degree of flexibility to fly properly. The exact amount of flex needed, though, is partially a function of the bow's draw weight or the power of the bow. If the arrow isn't flexible enough for the bow's draw weight, it could snap or shatter when the bow string is released. That's not a good thing and is likely to land you in the hospital.

This is why I stress taking your bow to a reputable dealer and having them help you determine the proper arrows for your purposes.

are designed and built, they have a finite and exact draw length. Recurves and longbows are more flexible and you can get away with shortening or extending the draw length a bit. Not so much with compounds. That said, most compound bows are somewhat adjustable so the user is able to change the draw length setting at least a bit. The mechanics of the bow are changed with the proper tools, adjusting the draw length to suit the archer.

Draw weight is another major factor in choosing a bow. The draw weight is a measurement of how much weight, in pounds, the archer needs to pull when drawing back the string. This can range from as little as 10 pounds for youth bows to upward of 60 pounds for larger compound bows. Remember, though, that with compound bows, the draw weight is roughly halved once the let-off point is reached. That's still 30 pounds, though, that needs to be held steady.

Draw weight is important for a couple of reasons. First, if the weight is too heavy, you will tire easily during practice. Second, if the weight isn't manageable for long periods of time, you'll have difficulty maintaining accuracy. That said, the more you practice, the more you'll improve your upper-body strength and, eventually, you may move up to a higher draw weight.

There is a substantial learning curve to achieve consistent accuracy. Don't get me wrong, archery is loads of fun and can be a great way to spend an afternoon. I'd hesitate, though, before recommending a bow and arrow as a feasible first line of home defense. Bows aren't small weapons, and they certainly aren't easy to conceal.

However, for those who are looking for a viable alternative to firearms for some sort of ranged weapon, the bow suits the bill nicely.

CROSSBOW

Ever since *The Walking Dead* became popular on TV, it seems like everyone and their brother wants a crossbow. Now, I'm not knocking the cool factor of the crossbow. It is a weapon I've admired since I was a young boy. Back then, I was really into comic books and there were a few different archery-based heroes, such as Green Arrow and Hawkeye. I always thought the comic book companies were missing the boat by not having a hero centered on the crossbow. Go figure, though. Combine the crossbow with zombies and, boom, instant popularity.

For the single-digit percentage of you out there who aren't familiar with a crossbow, it is simply a bow placed horizontally on a rifle stock. It is aimed and fired the same way one

Crossbow

would a rifle, though loading is a bit more laborious. The arrows for a crossbow are called quarrels, or bolts. For all intents and purposes, a crossbow bolt is nothing more than a short arrow. They average around 20 inches long. Each crossbow will note the proper length of bolt that should be used with it.

With most crossbows, loading a bolt is not a simple process. The crossbow will have a metal loop at the very front. This is called the stirrup. Place the stirrup on the ground, with the crossbow extending upward. Step into the stirrup with one foot to keep the crossbow in place. Then, using both hands, pull back on the string. Keep your thumbs running along the barrel as you pull. This will help you maintain even pressure on each side. Once the string locks into place, you can let go. Slide the bolt into the barrel and nock it on the string.

Even with practice, this is a time-consuming affair. Maybe that's why the comic book companies never explored the idea in any great detail.

It typically takes less practice to become proficient at the crossbow than with other bows. Traditional archery, even including the use of compound bows, takes considerable time, effort, and practice before consistent accuracy can be maintained. Crossbows also require practice, of course, but they tend to be slightly easier to learn. Plus, they are pretty cool.

WATER BALLOON SLINGSHOTS

There is a product on the market today that might be of interest to those who envision a return to some sort of medieval warfare at some point down the road. I've seen it called a few different things, but basically, it is a giant slingshot designed to launch water balloons at the beach. It takes three people to operate the slingshot. Two people grab the elastic bands, one on each side, and the third person pulls back and fires the projectile.

I can personally vouch for the power of these slingshots and have seen the range run a few hundred yards. With a little practice, these could be used to launch dangerous projectiles, such as Molotov cocktails (see page 147), at opponents far down the road. Precision shot placement isn't feasible with a water balloon slingshot, but with some practice, you'll be able to drop a projectile within about 5 to 7 feet of your target.

Pistol crossbows are the smaller cousins of the rifle-size ones. The pistol versions are essentially toys. They *might* work for hunting small game. But I would never consider them for any sort of real-world defense use.

As with the other types of bows, crossbows are an inferior choice compared to firearms but are viable options for thwarting an attacker. Not to mention they are great tools for when silence is desired.

SLINGS AND SLINGSHOTS

The sling is one of the oldest weapons known to man. It is extremely simple to make but can be difficult to master. The sling consists of a piece of material called a pouch with cordage extending from both sides. Traditionally, one of those cords ends in a loop and the other ends in a knot or a tab of some sort.

The length of the cordage can vary from sling to sling. Most often, the overall length of the sling, from end to end, is around 2 or 3 feet. The longer the sling, the greater the range it will have. Essentially, the sling acts as an extension of the throwing arm.

To use, a smooth stone is placed in the pouch. The cord with the loop is placed on a finger or thumb of the sling hand. The knot or tab on the loose end is then held in the same hand. The user gives the sling a fast overhand spin and releases the tab when the pouch is at the apex of the spin. The stone, at least in theory, flies forward and strikes the target. This takes practice— lots and lots of practice.

The slingshot is far easier to learn, and many a child has spent hours on end using one to shoot at tin cans and other targets. You've seen these in countless movies and cartoons even if you've never tried one your-self. It consists of a forked branch in the shape of a Y, with rubber bands running from the tops of the Y to a leather pouch. The rock or marble ammunition is placed in the pouch. The pouch is pinched between thumb and finger of one hand while the other hand holds the Y at the base. The pouch is pulled back, the shot aimed, and when the pouch is released, the ammunition flies forward. Modern versions use latex surgical tubing in place of rubber bands and an arm brace for stability.

Modern slingshots are quite powerful and can easily kill small game. As a defensive weapon, they may not be powerful enough to kill unless the shooter is exception-ally lucky or skilled. However, many guerrilla fighters have demonstrated the usefulness of the slingshot as a deterrent weapon. The slingshot, if sufficiently powerful, can be used to lob explosives and other nasties over walls and such, too.

If you attempt to use a slingshot for self-defense, con-centrate your aim on the face of the assailant. That's where you'll be able to do the most damage and cause the most pain. Ideally, keep the range under about 20 feet.

The downside to the slingshot is that the rubber bands or surgical tubes will degrade over time. Not only does this render the slingshot useless, but when one of those bands fails, it could snap back and injure the user.

The upside, though, is that ammunition for slings and slingshots is literally just about everywhere. Smooth stones work better than rough ones as they are less affected by wind. Marbles work great, as do large ball bearings. When practicing, hang an old blanket behind your targets. The blanket will keep you from losing all of your ammunition. Just be sure to leave the blanket loose at the bottom. If you hang the blanket too tight, your shots might just go right through the material.

BLOWGUNS

A blowgun would be a ridiculous weapon to rely on for defense. Seriously. Sure, they can be fun to play with in the backyard and, if you invest in a good-quality model, you can even use them to hunt squirrels and other small animals. About the only way a blowgun would be helpful to you in a defensive situation, though, is if it is sufficiently sturdy to use to beat the other guy senseless. A blowgun just doesn't generate enough power to be truly harmful to a human being. I don't care what you've seen in the movies. Pass on the blowgun.

• • •

Non-firearm projectile weapons are something to consider adding to your prepper arsenal. Bullets and gunpowder may one day run out. Or, for any one of several differ-ent reasons, you may not be allowed to possess or own a firearm. While a bow or slingshot are poor substitutes for a gun in a dangerous encounter, they sure beat empty hands.

CHAPTER 5
KNIVES

A knife is a tool, nothing more and nothing less. Granted, the same can be said of any other object discussed in this book. But, of all the different weapons discussed here, a knife is the one the average person will encounter on a daily basis, regardless of their background, job, or where they live. We use knives every single day, and many of us carry one or more of them in our pockets or on our belts.

I've been carrying a knife with me since I was about eight years old. Back when I was in school, most of us (the boys at least) carried a pocket knife and no one thought anything about it. Times have changed, of course. Yet even today, the only time you'll find me without a knife is if I'm at the airport or in some other restricted location.

Carrying a knife for the primary purpose of self-defense is a far different proposition than carrying one for opening boxes or whittling. Using a knife as a weapon, even in defense, requires a certain mindset, a determination, which firearms do not. With a handgun, you pull the trigger here and the bullet strikes the target over there. With a knife, though, this is up close and personal, folks. This is hearing them grunt as the knife slides in, smelling lunch on their breath as they exhale, feeling the slight resistance as the blade catches on their flesh, and feeling the splash of something hot and wet on your hand.

In other words, using a knife for defense isn't the best plan for everyone. If you decide to carry a blade, you need to come to terms with the reality that using it in that fashion is going to be ugly, brutal, and nothing like you see on TV.

There are thousands of different knives out there, many of them perfect candidates for a defensive weapon. I'm going to run through several things you'll want to consider as you choose the right blade for you. There is no way I can recommend any individual knife as being perfect for everyone. Ideally, as you shop around you'll have the opportunity to hold each knife in your hand and see how it fits. Given that most people order

Folding blade (left),
fixed blade (right)

online nowadays, that might not be feasible. Do yourself a favor, though, and stick to online stores that have a liberal return policy. Narrow your choices down to two or three knives and order them, then return the ones that you end up not liking for one reason or another.

FIXED VERSUS FOLDING

Once you've decided to carry a knife, your first choice is between a fixed blade or a folding blade. The folding knife tends to be smaller and more easily concealed. Of course, there are exceptions to that rule. There are truly massive folding knives and there are rather small fixed blades on the market. My personal dividing line is a blade length of 3 inches. Anything 3 inches or shorter works well as a folding knife. Anything longer and I'd rather it was fixed. Naturally, there are exceptions to that rule, too.

All other things being equal, a fixed blade is going to be stronger. Provided the knife is a full tang model, meaning the blade runs all the way through the handle as a single piece of metal, the fixed blade knife will withstand far more abuse than the folding knife. Plus, it lacks the moving parts that could become damaged and that could render a folding knife useless.

However, the fixed blade is typically a bit more difficult to conceal. A folding knife is also far more common in most people's day-to-day lives. If you're at the office and

KNIFE TERMINOLOGY

As you do your knife shopping, you'll no doubt run into a fair amount of jargon.

Spine: The edge of the knife opposite the sharpened side.

Butt: The base of the handle. The butt is at the opposite end of the knife from the tip. Many knives have a lanyard hole at the butt.

Jimping: A series of cuts or ridges that are often placed on the spine of the knife, typically near the handle. These provide grip for the thumb when doing fine cuts with the knife.

Swedge: On some blades, especially drop point and clip point (page 107), where the spine of the knife comes to the tip there will be a false edge of sorts. The blade will taper down and look almost like it is sharpened. This part of the spine is the swedge, and it serves to dramatically improve the piercing ability of the blade.

Belly: Most knives have a curve to the sharpened edge. This is the belly of the knife. The belly provides natural cutting action as the blade penetrates.

Scales: This is the material that is attached to the handle of the knife, typically through the use of adhesives, pins, or rivets. Some knives don't have scales and instead have cord wrapped around the handle.

Quillon: A curved section of the handle, either where the handle meets the blade, at the butt end of the knife, or both. The quillon prevents your hand from sliding up onto the blade or off of the handle when stabbing or pulling.

someone needs a sharp blade to cut open a box, which are you more likely to see used, a small folding knife or a fixed blade? If you hand someone a folding knife, even one that is rather robust, such as the Bad Monkey produced by Southern Grind or the Steel Will Apostate, most people won't think twice about it. But if you whip out an A. G. Russell Sting boot knife, your coworkers will be talking about it for weeks. Even though the Sting is a smaller knife, it is far more intimidating and just looks dangerous.

A folding knife blends in to most people's day-to-day lives and, therefore, is the more practical daily carry blade of choice for many. However, a fixed blade is generally a better choice for actual combat. The longer blade, coupled with the stronger design, will be more beneficial. That said, any blade is better than nothing at all.

Folding Knife Considerations

How the Knife Opens

When selecting a folding knife, one of your first considerations should be how the blade is opened. If you'll be relying on the knife for self-defense purposes, you should be able to open

The Steel Will Apostate (left) and the Kershaw Thermite (right) are two great tactical folders.

it with one hand. Fortunately, there are a few different knife designs that allow for this.

The first features a small thumb stud located on the spine of the blade. Holding the knife in your hand, you would use your thumb to push against the stud, opening the blade. Flicking the wrist once the blade is partially open will often speed up the process. Sometimes, a hole is used rather than a stud, but the same principle applies. The thumb pushes up against the hole, opening the knife.

The second design features a lever of sorts on the spine. Holding the knife in the hand and using the index finger to push down on the lever swings the blade open. This is my personal favorite design for one-handed opening.

The third design is called a wave, sometimes specifically an Emerson wave because Emerson Knives patented the feature. The wave is sort of a hook shape on the blade's spine. As you pull the knife from your pocket, this hook catches on the edge of the pocket

An example of an Emerson wave on a Bad Monkey folding knife from Southern Grind.

and swings the blade open. With practice, the knife opens almost automatically. This one seems to inspire a love it or hate it response. I know people who swear by the wave and others who swear *at* the wave because they've been cut more than once by the knife as it opens.

1.

2.

3.

4.

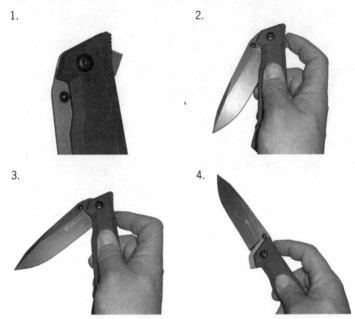

Opening a folding knife equipped with a lever or flipper is simple. Press the flipper while keeping your fingers away from the blade as it swings into place.

If possible, find at least one folding knife with each of the different options for opening and play around with them a bit. Get a feel for how they operate, and find the one that works best for you.

Blade Lock

Your chosen folding knife should have a blade lock. Otherwise, you run the risk of the blade folding closed on your fingers. There are two main types of locks for folding knives. Both will lock the blade in place as it opens fully.

- The lock back style has a button located at the back of the handle. Pressing this button releases the blade, and you use your other hand to fold it back into the handle.

- The liner lock is located inside the handle. Pushing the lock to the side frees the blade and allows it to fold into place.

Practice opening and closing, locking and unlocking your folding knife until it becomes second nature.

BUTTERFLY KNIVES

Sometimes called a balisong knife, the butterfly knife is illegal to carry in many parts of the country, but there are a few places where you won't get in trouble for having one. The butterfly knife is a folding knife where the handle is split and folds over to cover the blade. This type of knife became very popular in the United States the 1970s and 1980s, as they were often featured in many of the martial arts movies that were popular at the time.

Opening and closing the butterfly knife can be something of an art form. A skilled practitioner can flip the knife around and around as it clicks and clacks back and forth. However, in the real world, such theatrics aren't of much benefit.

Fixed Blade Considerations

Tang Options

There are three basic tang options for fixed blade knives. The full tang, as I mentioned before, is where the blade extends fully through the handle. This is the best option for a fighting knife as it makes the knife very strong. The rat tail tang, where the blade extends partly into the handle, is acceptable provided the steel and the knife construction as a whole are top quality. The third basic design is where the blade is mechanically attached to the handle, such as through the use of a bolt and nut. This last design isn't even a viable option, to be honest, when it comes to a fighting knife. Don't waste your money, no matter how cool the knife looks.

WHAT ABOUT SWITCHBLADES?

An automatic knife, commonly referred to as a switchblade, has a blade that either folds out from the side or slides out the front with the assistance of a spring-loaded button. You press the button and out comes the blade. These assisted opening knives are illegal to carry in many areas. While they are fun to play with and certainly look cool, out in the real world they aren't really worth the risk of getting caught with one. I can open my Kershaw Thermite folding knife just about as fast as any automatic knife and I won't run afoul of the law if I get caught with it in my pocket.

Single or Double Edge

Fixed blades come as either single or double edge. The single edge is just like every knife you have in your kitchen—one side of the blade is sharp, and the other is not. The double-edge design is what you'll find on many knives designed exclusively for fighting, where both sides of the blade are sharp. Now, here's the thing. A double-edge knife is very much a combat-oriented blade. It is designed for one thing and one thing only—to inflict damage. But that also limits its overall usefulness. You would find it difficult to use a double-edge knife effectively for most common survival tasks, such as processing firewood or skinning game.

Hand Guard

One design element I always look for is some sort of guard or hilt that protects the hand from the blade. At the minimum, I want the handle to be shaped such that it inhibits my fingers from sliding up to the sharp edge of the blade. Why do I feel this is important? Let's just say that when I was young, I did something really stupid when I was trying to show off for some friends

The Steel Will Darkangel is one of the most comfortable battle knives I've ever used.

and ended up with a pretty significant gash on one of my fingers.

A good example of a hand guard can be found on the Darkangel knife by Steel Will. The guard doesn't protrude far enough to be cumbersome, but it definitely protects the fingers from sliding up the blade when stabbing.

PUSH KNIVES

The push knife is a fixed blade design where the blade protrudes from the handle at a perpendicular angle. When holding the knife by the handle, the blade extends outward from between two fingers. Cutting or stabbing your attacker is as easy as punching. The blades on these knives are typically only a couple of inches long as they are meant to be easily concealed on the belt or boot,

The TOPS Grim Ripper push knife has a blade suitable both for thrusting and slashing, something not found in many other push knives.

or suspended on a neck chain. Push knives are often illegal to carry. One great example of a push knife is the Grim Ripper by TOPS Knives. It is a bit larger than the average push knife, with a blade just shy of 4 inches long. But that means it will go deeper into the target than other push knives, penetrating vital organs rather than just creating flesh wounds.

BLADE SHAPES

Knife designers have come up with innumerable blade shapes, or profiles, over the centuries. Each design has good points and bad points (no pun intended). Here are some of the more common ones.

Straight Back

The straight back is one of the simplest blade profiles. The top edge of the blade runs in a straight line from the handle to the tip. The sharpened edge has a good curve to it, giving it a lot of belly well-suited for slicing. The point is fairly strong but this is a knife made for cutting, not stabbing. The TOPS Street Scalpel is a good example of a straight-back blade.

The Bark River Knives Gunny is a typical straight-back blade.

Drop Point

The drop point is one of the most common blade profiles on the market today. The back of the blade is unsharpened and runs all the way to the tip in a slow arch. This make the point of the knife very strong. However, because the point

The Kershaw Injection 3.0 is an example of a drop-point blade profile.

is dropped somewhat, the knife isn't as adept at piercing as some of the other blade profiles. Because the drop-point design offers a curved belly, the knife is great for slicing and cutting. The Apostate by Steel Will is a great example of a drop-point blade.

Clip Point

The clip point, like the drop point, is immediately recognizable by most people. Quite often, the first knife people think of when they see this blade design is the classic bowie knife. With the clip point, the back of the blade extends straight out from the handle for about half the length of the blade. From there, the back of the blade dips down to the tip. This dip can either be curved or straight. Most often, this edge is left unsharpened, but I have seen sharpened

The bowie knife is a fine example of a clip-point knife.

ones from time to time. Either way, it is usually thinner along this edge than the rest of the blade's spine. What this blade shape does is provide a thin, sharp point that is excellent for piercing or stabbing. However, that same tip is weaker than the one on the drop-point blade. The clip-point blade usually has a good belly on it as well.

LANYARDS

Many fixed blade knives made today have a hole in the butt end of the handle for use with a lanyard. The idea of having a lanyard attached to your knife is so you won't lose the knife if it falls from your hand. Makes sense, right? Well, here's the thing. As with most things in life, there's a right way and a wrong way to use a lanyard. Never loop the lanyard around your wrist, especially if you're deploying the knife as a defense weapon. Keeping the lanyard looped around your wrist exposes you to serious risk.

Should you be lucky or skilled enough to use your knife effectively and stab your assailant, their normal reaction will be to turn away from the knife. As they do so, the knife will quite likely be pulled along with them. If your arm is attached to the knife by that lanyard, you'll be pulled along as well. At the least, you'll be pulled off balance. Worse, you might fall onto your assailant, which won't be nearly as fun as it sounds.

The proper way to use the lanyard is to put your thumb through the loop, then loosely wrap the lanyard around the back of your hand. If the knife falls from your grip, you'll still be able to hold the lanyard. But, if the knife is suddenly yanked away, your arm won't go with it.

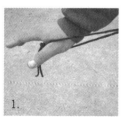

1. 2. 3.

Tanto

The tanto-style blade became wildly popular in the early 1980s due to the influence of knife manufacturer Cold Steel. Their advertisements showing a tanto knife stabbing through car doors and other obstacles without damage to the blade were found in all of the popular military, firearm, knife, and

A selection of tanto-style knives.

related magazines. The tanto design features sort of a squared-off look that leads to a very strong tip. Because of the almost chisel-like nature of the point, it can withstand abuse that would damage other blades. However, the blade itself is very straight and lacks any appreciable belly. This lack of a belly leads to it being used in more of a chopping motion, rather than slicing.

Spear Point

The spear point is what you often find on boot knives and other daggers. If you divide the

The CRKT Synergist (top) and the CRKT Sting (bottom) are both great options for an easily concealed defense knife.

blade in half where it meets the handle and run a line straight out from that point, that's where the tip of the spear point knife will be found. The edges of the blade are symmetrical. Quite often, both edges are sharpened, too, making it a double-edge knife. The tip of the spear point knife is very strong and is designed for penetration. The blade has a small belly on

Steel Will Adept 1000

each edge. Personally, I tend to favor knives that will be useful for common tasks as well as defense. However, if I were to carry a knife strictly for self-defense, I'd likely go with a spear point model, such as the CRKT Synergist. Another example is the Steel Will Adept 1000, which has a modified, squared-off spear point almost like a cross with a tanto blade shape.

TYPES OF STEEL

Once you've decided between fixed or folding and settled on a blade profile or shape, the next component is the steel. Steel is a metal made of iron mixed with carbon and other materials. The exact mixture determines the type of steel, of which there are literally thousands of permutations. Because there are so many variations, I'm only going to hit a few of the most common ones. The three most common categories you'll find in knives are carbon, stainless, and tool.

Carbon Steel

All steel has carbon. But blades designated as carbon steel have a touch more carbon than others. Carbon is the primary ingredient that gives steel its hardness. As mentioned, the harder the blade becomes, the less tough it will be. The other thing to remember with carbon steel is that it can rust easily if it isn't protected. Quite often, carbon steel blades will feature some sort of coating on them to protect against rust. The other option is to always remember to oil the blade after sharpening or use. Just a light coating of oil is all it takes to keep the knife in good shape.

Carbon steel is usually referred to by 10XX, where the XX represents the percentage of carbon in the steel. For example, 1095 is one of the most common carbon steels and the number means 0.95 percent of the steel is made of carbon. Many knife users prefer 1095 carbon steel because it holds an edge beautifully yet is still easy to sharpen.

Stainless Steel

Stainless steel has a high level of chromium. This element provides a great deal of corrosion resistance. Rust isn't typically an issue with stainless steel blades, nor is saltwater. If you live in a coastal area, stainless steel is going to be

HARDNESS AND TOUGHNESS

It is important to know that when it comes to steel, hardness and toughness are two distinctly different things. Hardness refers to how well the blade will hold an edge once it has been sharpened. The harder the blade, the less often you'll need to sharpen it. However, that same edge retention also means it can be difficult to sharpen. Toughness refers to the brittleness of the blade or how well it will hold up in normal use. As one increases, the other decreases. Meaning, a very hard steel will also be somewhat brittle. Steel is all about compromise and trying to find the balance you want between hardness and toughness.

your best bet. The tradeoff is that stainless steel isn't usually as tough as carbon steel. Among the most common of the stainless steels are the ones designated as 420 or 440. I'll tell you up front, if you come across a knife bearing a stamp of 420 on the blade, keep walking. It is a horrible choice for a knife. It doesn't retain an edge worth a darn. Once upon a time, 440 stainless steel was considered high end among knife customers. While it has been side-stepped by new steel formulas in recent years, 440 is still a solid choice.

Another somewhat common stainless steel is quite a mouthful—8Cr14MoV. There are slight variations, too, such as 8Cr13MoV and 8Cr15MoV. These tend to be fairly easy to sharpen, but they don't hold an edge very well.

Tool Steel

Tool steel is metal that has been formulated to be exceptionally wear-resistant as well as very hard. There are a few grades of tool steel you'll often find when knife shopping. The first, O1, has a high carbon content, close to 1 percent. It is rather prone to rust, so it needs to be properly cared for or protected. D2 tool steel has a lot of chromium, almost to the point of it being a stainless steel. D2 is very hard and will hold an edge, which is good because it will take a lot of work to put that edge on the blade. A2 tool steel is very tough and is often used in knife making for this reason.

Personally, I tend to favor carbon steel blades. I find most of them hold an edge very well, yet sharpening them isn't a chore. If you live in a wet environment, you may be better off with the stainless steel option. Tool steel can be a good choice but know going in that while they tend to hold an edge very well, sharpening tool steel blades can be difficult.

HANDLES

Assuming the knife has a full tang, the handle will consist of either some type of material that has been formed around the tang, such as poured plastic, or scales that are attached to the tang. Scales are thin pieces of material that are attached to the tang either mechanically using bolts or rivets or chemically using an adhesive.

One of the most common scale materials in use today is Micarta. This is a composite material composed of resin, linen, carbon fiber, paper, and other ingredients. The exact formula varies by manufacturer and intended use. It is a very hard material that holds up to a lot of abuse. Wood is another common material used for knife scales. Some of the most beautiful knife handles I've ever seen were made from wood.

It is important that the handle has some grip to it. A smooth handle may slip from your hand when it gets wet. Fortunately, most knife manufacturers provide handles that are easy to hold.

I tend to shy away from knives that have handles similar to brass knuckles. While they look cool, remember what I wrote earlier about lanyards? Same deal applies to handles where your fingers are sort of trapped. As for handle shape, this is truly a matter of personal preference. There are rounded, oval, and squared handles, with different contours available in each style. Find one that is comfortable for you.

RETENTION SYSTEMS

You need a way to carry your knife without risking injury to yourself. That's where the retention system comes into play. It allows you to attach the knife to your person in some way and keep the blade from damaging you or your stuff.

Sheaths can be made from a variety of materials but the most common, by far, are leather and Kydex. This latter is a type of plastic that starts out as a flat sheet and is then heated and molded around the knife (or other object) to fashion into a sheath. Personally, I'm something of a traditionalist and favor leather over other materials. But your mileage, as they say, may vary. Kydex is a great option for harsh environments.

It is important that no matter what type of sheath you use, it has some way of securely holding the knife in place. I know that sounds obvious, but I've seen many sheaths that didn't do a very good job of securing the knife. If the sheath is Kydex, the knife will likely snap into place. If leather, there will ideally be a loop or snap that keeps the knife secure.

For folding knives, many today have pocket clips attached. These clips serve to keep the knife easily accessible in your pocket. Rather than falling to the bottom of the pocket and forcing you to dig past loose change to get to it, the knife stays at the top of the pocket. I've found that clips as small as an inch or so in length still work great in this regard. Be forewarned, though, that new knives in particular will have very stiff clips and it can take some effort to remove them from the pocket.

No matter how you're carrying the knife, diligently practice pulling the knife until you can do it quickly and safely each and every time. Start slowly, of course. Practice the movements until they become muscle memory. It needs to become second nature, so you can do it without thinking.

KNIFE FIGHTING

Books, videos, even entire martial arts practices have been developed to teach people how to fight with a knife. Forget everything you've seen on TV and in the movies. Here's the brutal truth: if you're deploying your knife to save your life, close in on your assailant quickly, then slash and poke with the knife over and over until they go down. I'm serious as a heart attack. Hold the knife handle tight and try to inflict as much damage as possible as fast as you can. Then, run away even faster.

If you want to explore knife fighting beyond that, find a local Kali or Eskrima school. They will teach you far more than you'll learn from any book.

Many people carry knives on a daily basis but the intent is for them to be used as tools rather than weapons. Using a knife to intentionally harm another human being takes a certain mindset and commitment. While certainly intimidating to most attackers, a knife brandished without the intent to use it may quickly be taken away and used against you.

CHAPTER 6

MELEE WEAPONS

First things first, what is a melee weapon? The word "melee" refers to close quarters combat. Think within arm's reach or thereabouts. A melee weapon is used in close proximity to your attacker. The term "melee weapon" first came into common use in the 1980s when role playing games like Dungeons and Dragons became popular.

There are two categories of melee weapons: blunt and bladed.

BLUNT WEAPONS

These are weapons that cause impact injuries, for the most part. We're not slicing and dicing, we're striking and bruising. Make no mistake, though, these weapons can be just as deadly as their bladed counterparts.

Brass Knuckles

Just about everyone is familiar with brass knuckles, if only at a visual level. This is a weapon that serves two purposes. First, it increases the level of injury your assailant receives from a  punch. Second, it helps to protect your own hand from injuries sustained from punching your attacker. For those who have never had to do it, punching someone can injure your own hand, especially if you strike your opponent's face.

Brass knuckles are rarely made from brass, of course. In fact, many modern versions are made out of plastic. I prefer metal, though, as the weight of it adds strength to the punch. I've seen some variations, too, that include spikes, blades, and other embellishments to the traditional brass knuckles. To each their own, I guess, but those spikes and such are just as likely to snag on clothing and trap your hand as they are to cause serious injury to your attacker.

Clubs and Batons

One of the oldest weapons known to man is the stick. Over the centuries, we've come up with all sorts of ways to modify the basic stick and make it a far more formidable weapon.

Batons, in one form or another, have been used by law enforcement officers since the early 1800s. Since they were first introduced, they've gone through changes in shape and size, going from what was essentially a small club to a longer weapon used for leverage-based holds as well as striking to expandable versions that take up far less space on a duty belt.

Police-style baton

Batons work well as hand-held impact weapons, but other than the expandable models, they are somewhat difficult to carry concealed. Expandable batons have a few quirks, too. The tip of the baton, when deployed, is far thinner than the handle. This means most of the weight of the weapon is in your hand, rather than evenly distributed along the length. The result is strikes that aren't as forceful as they may otherwise be. Also owing to the collapsible design, you can't use the tip of the baton for poking or prodding your assailant. Doing so may result in the baton collapsing back into the handle. The embarrassment at that happening may be the least of your worries.

For home defense, if you lack a firearm, a club such as a baseball bat will serve nicely. Keep in mind that while swinging for the cheap seats will certainly do the job if you connect, if you miss you'll likely spin yourself right into the ground. Poking the bat into the solar plexus works rather well. I'm not saying to avoid going for the head shot, just that there are many ways to skin the proverbial cat.

The baseball bat can also be easily carried in a vehicle without undue suspicion. Buy an old baseball glove and a ball or two at a thrift store and toss them in the  back seat with the bat. No one will think twice about seeing it in there.

Blackjacks and Saps

While these weapons were once ubiquitous, at least as far as TV and movies were concerned, we don't see them a whole lot today. Despite the fact that the terms are often used interchangeably, blackjacks and saps are actually slightly different from one another.

The sap is a flat weapon, often made of leather, with a piece of metal running from end to end inside the leather. The metal inside is thin enough to provide a spring action. The striking end is sometimes weighted with powdered lead.

The blackjack is very similar in design but it is usually cylindrical in shape, rather than flat. It usually has a standard coiled spring inside as well, rather than just a thin piece of metal. Like the sap, it may be weighted with powdered lead or another material.

As should be obvious, the sap or blackjack is used to strike the assailant, usually in the head. The way the weapons are constructed, they provide a forceful blow to the head without damaging the scalp, resulting in unconsciousness without having to worry about blood. Both weapons are often prohibited by law, but they are very effective.

If you shop around, you can often find variations of this type of weapon hidden in everyday objects, such as ball caps and gloves.

Sjambok

This weapon is a stout whip, usually 3 to 5 feet in length. It is made of a thick material, traditionally hippopotamus hide, though plastic ones are easily found. When one thinks of a whip, they tend to imagine Indiana Jones and his famous bullwhip. There are, however, a few different kinds of whips, of which the sjambok is merely one. The sjambok is very common in South Africa, where it is used to defend against animals as well as people.

In use, the sjambok is swung like a baton or rod. There is no flicking of the wrist like you'd do when cracking a bullwhip. The sjambok increases your reach, allowing you to strike your attacker at a bit of a distance. The wounds inflicted by a sjambok can be quite severe.

Canes and Walking Sticks

I differentiate batons from canes by length. If it is short enough that you'd regularly carry it on your belt or in your hand, it is a baton. However, if it reaches from your hand to the ground while standing, it is a cane or walking stick.

Canes come in a variety of sizes and shapes. The models that have a hooked or angled handle allow you to add trapping maneuvers to your repertoire, with practice. Canes and walking sticks are often just a little too long for one-handed strikes, though with the adrenaline pumping, you could probably pull it off once or twice. A better tactic, though, is to use two hands and utilize the cane as a short staff, flicking an end to strike your attacker or using the cane to block incoming blows.

Test out different lengths until you find the one that is most comfortable for you. A good starting point is half of your height in inches. Another approach is to stand up straight and have your arms relaxed at your sides. Have someone else use a tape measure and find the distance from your wrists to the floor. Neither of these methods is foolproof, of course, but both can give you an idea of where to begin your search.

Sword canes are a real thing, too. You've seen them in countless old movies, I'm sure. The hero will be walking down some dark cobblestone side street late in the evening. When he's accosted by some ruffian, he slides a hidden sword from his cane and makes short work of the bad guy. In the real world, sword canes are neat but are often

Cane sword handle

Opening a cane sword

very cheaply made. The metal used for the blades is rather soft and won't take or keep an edge very well. Sword canes are also illegal in many areas and, even where legal, are often considered a concealed weapon and are thus subject to all of those restrictions.

Of course, a sword cane is a cross between a blunt melee weapon and a bladed one, which serves as a great segue into the next topic.

BLADED WEAPONS

I talked about knives in a previous chapter. Here, I'm going to discuss long blades as well as other weapons that have sharp edges. I cannot stress the importance of training and practicing with these weapons. While any weapon is dangerous to an inexperienced user, blades carry with them a little more risk than a club or sap.

Machete

A machete is the bridge between a knife and a sword. The average machete blade runs around 12 to 18 inches. They are, first and foremost, tools used for clearing brush and such. They are designed to be used single-handedly, usually with broad strokes back and forth. Make no mistake, it can be quite a workout to blaze a trail through thick undergrowth with a machete.

There are many types or styles of machetes, most of which are regional in origin. One of the most common variations has a wider blade toward the tip, adding a little extra weight and strength to each swing. You'll find this on the panga and bolo styles. Taking this a step further, the kukri-style

Machete

machete puts an angle on the blade itself in addition to widening the tip. The kukri originates in Nepal where it is a very common working knife. Many in the Western world were first introduced to the kukri when it was used by Jonathan Harker to slice open Dracula's throat in the original Bram Stoker novel. Having used my Cold Steel kukri for a couple of years now, I can say that it is a fearsome tool that takes a beating and keeps looking for more.

A machete could do some serious damage in a fight, that's for certain. Effective use, though, does require some room to move. While you need to be up close and personal with your attacker, you need space to swing, playing to the weapon's advantages.

Spear

A spear is essentially just a stick with some sort of sharp point on one end. Said point might be made of metal or plastic, or it could just be the spear shaft itself whittled down and hardened in a fire. I would caution you, though, against just attaching a butcher knife to the end of a broom handle and calling it a day. First, the balance of the weapon is likely not going to be ideal. Second, you stand a pretty good chance of that knife detaching from the spear at the most inopportune time.

A spear is sort of two weapons in one, both a staff and a blade. That's the good news. The bad news is they can be awkward to use, especially in close quarters like a hallway. Jabbing and thrusting work great, provided the other person doesn't manage to grab the shaft and pull you off balance.

For practical purposes, forget all about throwing the spear at your attacker. That'd just be foolish, especially indoors. Personally, if I were to choose a spear as a defense weapon, I'd go with one that had a shaft of around 3 feet. That would be much easier to use in tight spaces, yet still give me the extra reach I might want or need.

Tomahawk

The tomahawk was invented by Native Americans, specifically the Algonquian. A stone with a sharp edge was attached to the end of a wooden handle and used in combat as well as for every day chores like processing firewood. European settlers replaced the stone head with a metal one, vastly increasing the durability of

The SOG Tactical Tomahawk is a modern evolution of the Vietnam tomahawk.

the weapon. Over time, the design of the tomahawk has changed a bit, specifically with regard to the poll, or the side of the tomahawk's head that is opposite the sharp blade. Some models include a spiked poll; others have more of a hammer head.

The size of the blade differs from model to model, too. A tomahawk designed to be at least somewhat historically accurate will have a longer edge than a so-called tactical one. The latter style of tomahawk isn't meant for chopping firewood and is intended primarily for combat use as well as defending against forced entry situations.

One thing to bear in mind when using a tomahawk against a human being is it might very well stick where it hits, especially if the blade is fairly short. While adrenaline will likely help you yank it free, don't count on it coming out easily.

Karambit

The karambit originated in Southeast Asia and has since spread throughout much of the world. While I could have included this weapon in the chapter on knives, it differs enough from the traditional knife that I felt I should include it here instead. The karambit has a curved blade and resembles an animal claw. I have come across models where both edges of the blade are sharpened and other models where it is only the inner edge that cuts.

The Karambit originated in Indonesia.

The karambit's handle will have a hole at the butt end. Traditionally, the karambit is held such that the blade comes down from the bottom of the fist and curves outward. Held in this way, the index finger is inserted through the hole in the handle. Some people prefer to hold it in what is sometimes called a hammer fist grip, where the blade extends from the top of the fist, the same way you'd hold a standard knife when working in the kitchen or something. In that case, it is the pinky finger that goes through the hole in the handle.

Owing to the wicked curve to the blade, the karambit is capable of doing serious damage to an attacker. Because of the design of the handle, it is difficult to disarm someone who is using a karambit. Some models add a bit of a spiked flourish to the handle on the outside of the finger hole. This gives you the option of punching with the weapon as well as slashing.

I'd consider the karambit to be a backup weapon rather than anything I'd rely on right off the bat. It is a fearsome weapon, no question, but I'd rather use a weapon that will keep some distance between me and the attacker, if possible.

• • •

Melee weapons, whether blunt or bladed, pale in comparison to firearms. But, they can be a viable option for those who are unable or unwilling to use a boom stick. The weapons in this chapter will all do quite a bit of damage to an attacker and most of them require minimal training to become effective if not proficient with them.

CHAPTER 7
MARTIAL ARTS WEAPONS

Time and again throughout this book, I've stressed the importance of training prior to using weapons. This is especially important with weapons coming from the world of martial arts, which, used improperly, will be ineffective at best and injurious to the user at worst.

I have to be honest. Many martial arts weapons aren't very practical for modern-day use in the real world. I mean, it isn't like you're going to strap a sword to your back for your daily commute to the office. If you do that regularly and get away with it, you have a way more awesome job than I do, that's for sure.

Martial arts weapons do have a high cool factor, though. Plus, and this is actually pretty important to understand, proficiency with these weapons translates into a great degree of self-confidence as well as increasing your physical fitness. You'll burn far more calories practicing with a staff or tonfa (see page 137) than you will by plinking targets at the range.

There are hundreds if not thousands of different martial arts weapons. Indeed, just about every martial art in existence utilizes at least a few different ones, though they are often variations on a theme. For example, Okinawan karate has the nunchaku, a weapon very much associated with Bruce Lee. However, Lee likely learned at least the basic techniques by practicing with a different weapon,

WHAT IS A MARTIAL ART?

Man has been beating the hell out of one another since well before we discovered fire. During those thousands of years, we've developed more than a few ways to do it. Over time, we've decided to use the term "martial art" to refer to any sort of at least semiorganized system for inflicting harm on another human being using either body weapons such as hands and feet or handheld weapons like swords and sticks. Quite often, when we hear the term "martial arts," we immediately think of karate, judo, kung fu, and the like. Those all originated in East Asia and the image of two or more people kicking and wrestling while wearing loose, white uniforms is ubiquitous, even if it isn't always technically accurate. It is important to realize that every corner of the globe has its own native fighting arts and styles. Examples include:

East Asia (Japan, China, Korea, etc.): judo, ninjutsu, karate, kung fu, tae kwon do

Philippines: eskrima, arnis, kali

the tabak-toyok, which originates with the Philippine martial arts.

In this chapter, I'm going to run through seven of the more common martial arts weapons. A few of them you can actually make yourself with a little ingenuity once you understand how the weapon is used. Bear in mind, though, that possession of some of these weapons outside of the home or a martial arts school may be illegal. Be sure to do your homework before carrying any of these weapons for

Europe: wrestling, fencing

Middle East: krav maga

South America: capoeira, Brazilian jujitsu

North America: American kenpo (or kempo), to-shin do, jailhouse rock

That's just a snapshot. There are thousands of different fighting styles in existence. The vast majority of them include a weapons component in the training process. Some arts like eskrima are very weapons-oriented while others include weapons only at the higher levels of training. Do some searching in your area and find out what martial arts arc being taught locally. Even if that particular art or school doesn't teach the weapons that are of most interest to you, martial arts training in general will help you in many ways, including increasing your physical fitness as well as your situational awareness.

self-defense, lest you find yourself in hot water with local authorities.

One more thing. If you decide to purchase a martial arts type of weapon, shop around carefully. There is a lot of junk out there—weapons that look pretty or cool but lack any sort of durability or craftsmanship. As mentioned, training in the use of these weapons is crucial. Your trainer or instructor should be able to recommend a reliable source for good-quality weapons.

STICK

One of the oldest weapons known to man is the stick. Just about every martial art that has a weapons component will include stick training. Here's the thing, though. Different arts use different stick lengths. Some arts, such as Eskrima, favor shorter sticks around 30

Bo staff

inches in length. Other arts, such as traditional karate, use the bo staff, which runs almost 6 feet long. As techniques evolved in different martial arts over the course of hundreds of years, each art began to concentrate on specific lengths for their staves and batons.

The stick or staff can be a very effective weapon, provided you know how to use it. It is also extremely easy to carry such an innocuous weapon. Using a cane doesn't necessarily require mobility issues. Plus, every hiker can use a good walking stick, though those tend to be a big longer than the traditional cane.

Personally, I'm not keen on the canes that have hidden swords or other weaponry. In the vast majority of cases, the hidden weapon is of very poor quality and the item is truly just a novelty for show rather than meant for actual use.

I've found a length of about 40 to 42 inches is ideal for me for most uses, though I've played around with both shorter and longer staves over the years. As with many other weapons, a lot of this is a matter of personal preference and comfort. A longer staff means extra weight. This means more strength is necessary to wield it effectively, but it also adds power to a strike. I tend to be able to strike faster with a moderate length staff than I do with a full bo staff.

NUNCHAKU

The nunchaku (sometimes spelled nunchuku and often referenced as "nunchucks" or even "numchucks") is a deceptively simple weapon. Traditionally, it consists of two sticks, each roughly 1 foot long, connected by a few inches of rope or chain. There are numerous variations, too, such as longer or shorter sticks, longer rope or chain, and even the addition of a third stick to the mix. Mentioned earlier, the tabak-toyok is similar to the nunchaku but the sticks are shorter, roughly 4 to 8 inches or so, and the chain is longer, around 6 or 7 inches. Like socks or pants, the weapon is usually referred to as a pair of nunchaku.

The basic operation of the nunchaku involves holding one stick in the hand and swinging the other stick to strike the opponent. There are several different basic moves and strikes. Most of them, though, are just slightly different ways of swinging the weapon, such as overhand, underhand, and using different grips on the sticks. That's not meant to imply the weapon is easily learned or that there is little skill involved in its use.

Nunchaku

In properly trained hands, the nunchaku can be devastatingly lethal. In untrained hands, well, search YouTube for "nunchaku fails." A word of warning, though. Don't drink anything while checking out some of those videos as you may risk damaging your keyboard with a spray of water or soda.

A pair of nunchaku can be easily concealed on your person, especially if you're wearing a long shirt or coat and slip the nunchaku into your waistband. However, effective use of the nunchaku requires some freedom of movement. This isn't a weapon you can use in a confined space.

TONFAS

The tonfa is a baton type of weapon at times referred to as a "side handle baton." For many years, police officers carried a version of the tonfa as their standard baton, called a PR-24. The tonfa consists of a straight stick with a handle attached at a right angle near one end. Traditionally, the tonfa is sized

Tonfa

to the user so when the handle is gripped and the longer portion of the stick rests along the forearm, the end of the stick should extend an inch or so beyond the elbow.

Proper use of the tonfa can actually be somewhat complex owing to the numerous grips and techniques one can employ. It is a weapon equally suited for offense and defense. In the martial arts, the tonfa is traditionally used in pairs. The law enforcement variant, though, is used singly.

When gripped by the handle such that the long stick rests against the bottom of the forearm, the tonfa can be used defensively to block an attack. It can also be thrust forward into an opponent or thrust backward as though it were an extension of an elbow to strike someone behind you. The baton can also be held by the grip and spun outward to strike an opponent. Held by the end of the long stick, the handle could be used to hook an opponent's arm or leg.

Given the size of the tonfa at well over 1 foot in length, concealing the weapon could prove to be problematic. It is a very versatile weapon, though, and one worth considering if martial arts weapons are of interest to you.

KUBOTAN

Very much like how Kleenex, a trademarked name, has become a term for tissues, Kubotan has become a generic name for keychain weapons similar in size and shape to pens. It all started with Takayuki Kubota. A lifelong student of the martial arts, Kubota had earned black belts in several styles, such as judo, aikido, and karate. In the late 1960s, Kubota developed the

Kubotan

Kubotan. It is a plastic, baton-shaped weapon about 5 inches long and ½ inch thick.

Once the Los Angeles Police Department began training their female officers in the use of the Kubotan in the

1970s, the weapon's popularity skyrocketed. Since that time, there have been innumerable copycat weapons, many of them using the Kubotan name despite having no affiliation with the trademarked product.

The Kubotan, as well as its imitators, is clenched in the fist and used to either strike or to press hard against vulnerable areas of the body, such as the small of the back or the side of the neck. Knowledge of the body's pressure points greatly increases the efficacy of the Kubotan.

Given the small size, the Kubotan is well-suited to carry just about anywhere, though I'd think twice about walking

SHURIKEN

One of the most recognizable weapons from the martial arts universe, the shuriken is commonly referred to as a throwing star. In countless movies, black-clad ninja are  portrayed assassinating victims from afar with a simple toss of these spinning wheels of death. That, of course, is all Hollywood nonsense.

In reality, shuriken were tools of distraction. Occasionally, they may have been laced with poisons or infectious material, such as animal dung. But, by and large, they weren't used to kill, but only to distract and annoy pursuers.

While they are loads of fun to toss at foam targets and such, their use as a weapon in the real world is minimal at best.

into a courthouse or other similarly secured building with one. This weapon in particular truly requires training and practice to implement effectively.

KUSARI-FUNDO

The kusari-fundo, in some arts called a manrikigusari, is one of the simplest weapons in this chapter. It consists of a length of chain with a weight on each end. The length of the chain varies, typically a minimum of 1 foot and up to 3 or 4 feet in length. The longer the chain, the more difficult it can be to control. In my experience, around 2½ to 3 feet is ideal.

The chain is typically not extremely thick or robust. Thick chains are heavy and the kusari-fundo is meant to be light enough to swing around without too much trouble. At the same time, though, it shouldn't so thin it is easily broken. That would defeat the purpose, right?

Extremely concealable, the chain can be tossed into a jacket or pants pocket with little difficulty. The weapon is also very easy to improvise. Buy a length of chain and affix a small padlock to each end of it. If it were found in your possession and you were questioned about it, the chain could just as easily be a bike lock as a weapon. In fact, I know one guy who habitually wears a chain like a necklace under his shirt. Rather than padlocks, he has extra-large links on each end. The chain is hardly noticeable unless you're actually looking for it.

If you decide to make a kusari-fundo yourself, head to the hardware store for the chain. Many hardware stores sell chains by the foot in various types and sizes. Examine the different chains and find one that isn't too heavy and is also very flexible. Avoid chains that have links that seem to lock up when twisted, such as the chains often used for dog runs.

The kusari-fundo is a close-range weapon that can be used in several different ways. Held and swung, the weapon can strike an assailant with one of the weighted ends, causing blunt force injuries. The chain can be used to snare or trap an arm or leg, or even to strangle the aggressor.

SWORD

Of all of the weapons discussed in this chapter, the sword is probably the most difficult to use properly. It takes years of training to become even somewhat skilled with a sword. Without such training and practice, the sword is cumbersome and difficult to employ with any real degree of effectiveness. Too many people swing them like they are essentially thin, sharpened baseball bats or something. If someone gets inside that swing, the sword becomes more of a hindrance than a help.

Don't get me wrong, though. In the hands of an experienced user, a sword can be a fiercely lethal weapon. It does require a little elbow room; this isn't a weapon you'd be able to use in close quarters. However, there are many different lengths and styles of swords available, allowing the user to find one that best suits their typical environment as well as their body size and fighting skill set.

While I believe swords are a less-than-ideal choice for a weapon in most situations, if push came to shove I'd favor something on the shorter end of the spectrum. The longer the sword, the more difficult it is to wield. A short sword, such as the Roman Gladius, gives the user more options when it comes to close spaces. Plus, a short sword can often be used with just one hand, leaving the other free for grappling, keeping balance, or other needs.

A sword is not going to be readily concealed, despite what you may have seen in the movies or on TV. Even if a long duster were to hide your ninja sword, drawing it from the scabbard would be difficult. If a sword figures into your defense plans, you're far better off having it be something you're using at home or at the retreat rather than when you're out and about, at least during normal times. After some sort of societal collapse and we've all gone Mad Max, there may indeed be a revered spot for the sword in your daily carry arsenal.

CHAPTER 8

HOMEMADE WEAPONS

You don't need to be MacGyver to cobble together a few weapons from stuff you have sitting around the house. In fact, a few of the weapons I'm going to discuss in this chapter don't even need to be built. It's more accurate to say you'll be modifying a common item for defensive purposes.

Keep in mind that just about anything can be used as a weapon, provided sufficient force or creativity are applied. I'm going to cover some of the more obvious options. Feel free to see what you can come up with on your own.

DEFENSIVE SPRAYS

Pepper spray is widely available and not very expensive. However, there may be times when you need to come up with an alternative. For years, various experts have suggested using wasp and hornet spray. It has a great range, up to about 20 feet, and because it is a stream rather than an aerosol, it is easy to direct. The problem, though, is that most of those sprays are specifically designed to affect the nervous systems of insects. This would expose users to some legal liability, as the can specifies that using the product in a manner inconsistent with the labeling can be a violation of federal law.

That said, here's one recipe for homemade pepper spray that will definitely catch an assailant's attention:

Ingredients:

- 2 tablespoons of thinly sliced peppers

- 1 cup or so of isopropyl alcohol (rubbing alcohol)

- Several drops of baby oil

Materials:

- Latex or vinyl gloves

- 2 glass jars with lids

- Coffee filter

- Funnel

- Spray bottle

I cannot stress the importance of gloves enough. No matter how careful you are, you will end up getting pepper oil on your hands. This can be difficult to wash off completely. You'll realize that later when you use the bathroom.

The hotter the peppers, the better. Cayenne pepper will certainly work, and most people have it in their spice rack in the kitchen. You could visit the grocery store and pick up a couple of chili peppers, too. Or, if you feel particularly brave, seek out a bhut jolokia, or ghost pepper. That, my friend, is one of the hottest peppers known to man. Handle with care.

While wearing your gloves, fill one glass jar with about two tablespoons of peppers. If you're using whole peppers from the store, cut them up first. Slice them thin so as to expose as much of the pepper's oil as possible. Pour in enough of the alcohol to completely cover the pepper to a depth of about half an inch or so. Being careful to avoid splashing, gently stir this mixture for a few minutes.

Add several drops of baby oil, then seal the lid on the jar, and shake it up. Make sure the lid is on tight. As an added precaution, you may want to hold a dish towel around the jar's lid as you shake, in case of leakage. The baby oil helps to thicken the mixture just a touch and also helps the spray stick to the skin.

Keep your face well away as you open the jar. The odor that comes out will not be pleasant. Pour the mixture through a coffee filter into the other jar. This will remove the solids that could cause trouble in your spray bottle.

Then, use the funnel to pour the filtered liquid into your spray bottle. Carefully dispose of the coffee filter and peppers.

The spray bottle can be one you've picked up at the dollar store or the health and beauty department of your local discount retailer. Make sure you label the bottle clearly, and keep it well away from children. Consider tying a piece of string around the bottle, and then covering the string with a strip of duct tape. This will make it very easy to tell which spray bottle you have in your hand, even in the dark, as you'll be able to feel that string. The tape is there to keep the string from falling off.

The spray bottle will have a variable setting on the nozzle, from a fine mist to a stream. Keep it set to the latter. You're not going to have a huge range with it, perhaps 10 feet, so keep that in mind. Take it outside for a few test sprays so you're familiar with the range and how the stream shoots. Homemade pepper spray isn't nearly as effective on the skin as it is in the eyes, so that's where you want to aim.

The spray won't remain viable forever. You'll need to mix a new batch every few weeks. But that's a small price to pay if this is your best option for having pepper spray on hand.

MOLOTOV COCKTAIL

This incendiary weapon is simplicity itself to make.

1. Start by finding a container, such as a bottle or jar. It is important that the container is glass and not plastic. It needs to shatter upon impact. In terms of size, even a relatively small container, such as a beer bottle filled with fuel, will create a good-size fire.

2. Fill your breakable bottle or jar with a flammable liquid, such as gasoline, turpentine, or alcohol. The fuel can be thickened through the addition of other substances. This makes the fuel sticky and far more dangerous. It's bad enough to get splashed with burning gasoline, but when it sticks to an attacker's clothing and skin, it will turn a bad day far worse. Common additives include Styrofoam, dish soap, and motor oil.

3. Attach a wick of sorts to the outside of the container, traditionally by using the bottle's stopper. The wick can be any combustible material, such as a strip of cotton from old T-shirts. If the stopper or cap for the bottle is unavailable, stuff

one end of the wick down into the bottle, wrap the loose end around the bottle's mouth a time or two, then secure with duct tape or rubber bands.

4. Light the wick and throw the container. Dipping the wick in kerosene or another flammable liquid beforehand will make it easier to light, and help it stay lit as it sails through the air. The wick is sometimes partially stuffed down into the neck of the bottle, but this isn't necessary. The wick doesn't act as a fuse. Instead, the wick ignites the fuel only after the bottle smashes.

5. Upon impact, the bottle will shatter. The lit wick will ignite the liquid, creating a fireball from the droplets in the air as well as spreading the fire as the liquid splashes around.

Obviously, this isn't a weapon you'd use indoors or on anyone who is near your home. Rather, a Molotov cocktail would be used against groups of assailants before they reach your front door. Bear in mind, though, that by sending out one or more of these bottles of improvised napalm, you are also giving your attackers fire that could be used against you. For example, they could light their own improvised torches from the fire you've given them and send them back in your direction.

Another word of caution. It will be very easy for someone to see a Molotov cocktail flying through the air, especially at night. Not only might they be able to get out of the way before impact, they could visually backtrack the path right to where you're hunkered down. If that could pose problems, you might want to try a different tactic.

HAIRSPRAY FLAMETHROWER

This is one many of us have made in the past, particularly as youngsters. Depress the button on a can of aerosol hairspray and hold a lit match in front of the spray and, voila, you have an instant flamethrower.

While kind of cool to watch, the practical uses of this weapon are fairly limited. The flame doesn't shoot very far and isn't very concentrated. It's more like a cloud of flame than a stream. Using it outdoors will put you at risk for stray wind currents, which could send the flame back at you.

Something interesting to note about using fire for defensive purposes: Once someone is set alight, they don't tend to sit still. Instead, they will, for the most part, run around willy nilly. Sure, a few of them might remember to implement the old stop, drop, and roll technique. Either way, you run the risk of them spreading the fire as they very understandingly panic and run amok. Consider this fair warning: Use fire with extreme caution.

MODIFIED BASEBALL BAT

A baseball bat is a fairly formidable weapon in its own right. Wood or aluminum, a smack or two with this weapon will dissuade many an attacker. However, with just a little work, you can take the lethality of the bat to the next level.

The first thing that usually comes to mind is to drive some nails through the thick end of a wooden bat. The problem with doing so is the nails tend to stick into the person you hit. Rather than impacting the body or face and releasing, the bat may catch and hold. While the damage done to the person will no doubt be severe, you may be knocked off balance or have the bat torn from your hands.

Instead, try this. Take several glass soda or beer bottles and smash them up in the bottom of a bucket. Be sure to use eye protection and gloves. You don't need the glass pounded into dust, but break up any pieces that are larger than a couple of inches across. Use a sledgehammer to firmly pound on the glass. There's no need to swing the hammer like you're chopping firewood. Cover the last several inches of the thick of the bat with adhesive, such as epoxy or even hot glue, then dip it into the bucket of glass. If you're using hot glue, you may have to do it in sections, otherwise the glue may harden before you're able to cover the entire thing.

The addition of glass shards obviously increases the amount of damage you'll do to another person when using the bat as a weapon. This also takes you beyond the "heat of the moment" in the eyes of the law. If you keep a standard baseball bat in your backseat, along with a couple of baseballs and a mitt or two, an argument could be made that you just happened to have it with you at the time of the incident and grabbed it on your way out of the car. Few people are going to use a glass-encrusted bat for softball practice.

Modifying the bat in this way also means you'll need to be careful about storing it. If you think stubbing your toe on an end table is painful, imagine your toe meeting the working end of this bat an hour before sunrise. One solution is to use a small cardboard box. Put the box on the floor in the corner behind your front door, for example, and put the bat in it, not unlike how you'd use an umbrella stand.

SLUNGSHOT

No, that isn't a typo. The slung-shot is a distinctly different weapon from the slingshot. It has its origins in the maritime world. The slungshot consists of a weight attached to the end

of a rope or other piece of cordage. Often, the weight was called a monkey fist, which is a woven knot surrounding a ball bearing or something similar. The slungshot was used when mooring boats. It was attached to the line on a boat and tossed over to someone on a pier. The weight of the slungshot made it easier to throw. The person on the pier would then reel in the line, pulling the boat into position.

To make one at home for use as a weapon, simply take a piece of thin rope, such as a clothesline, and tie a 2-inch-long bolt to one end. Thread a few large nuts onto the rope, snugging them down against the bolt. Then, tie a knot behind the nuts to keep them in place. Tie one or two large knots at the other end of the rope. I like to have a total length of about 2 feet from end to end.

To use, hold the non-weighted end in your hand, and let the weight dangle toward the ground, then swing the rope like a flail at your target. Don't spin it around like you're a cowboy in the Old West about to lasso a runaway horse. The knots on the non-weighted end of the rope give you something to hold so the rope doesn't slide out of your hand.

There are innumerable variations on this basic design, particularly as to what is used for the weight on the end of the rope. There are several videos online that show how to tie the traditional monkey's fist knot, if you want to go that route. Otherwise, anything hard and a bit heavy will work, provided it is securely attached to the rope. Examples include small pieces of wood or junk metal from a scrap yard. It might take some experimentation to get the weight just right. Too heavy and the rope will be clumsy and difficult to swing accurately. Too light and you risk not doing very much damage to your opponent.

ROCK IN A SOCK

The rock in a sock is rather similar to the slungshot. This weapon is made just like it sounds, by putting rocks or some other heavy object into a sock. Obviously, you don't want to use an ankle sock for this. Instead, use a sock that is at least calf high or longer. Tube socks work great. The rocks should be a little larger than golf balls and you only need two or three of them. Much more than that and the weapon will be awkward to swing due to the weight.

In place of rocks, consider using a couple of old D batteries. I've found that's just about the perfect amount of weight. I tape them together side by side with duct tape before dropping them into the sock. There's no real tactical advantage in doing so, I just think it makes things neat and tidy.

Other options for weights include gravel, nuts and bolts, or golf balls. Use whatever is available to you. The only caveat I'd offer is if you use objects with sharp or rough edges, over time you may find holes developing in the sock.

Tie a knot in the sock to keep the rocks or other weights at the toe end. To use, wrap the loose end of the sock around your hand, then swing the weighted end at the target.

Making weapons at home from stuff you have around the house can actually be fun. It gets the creative juices flowing. What is important to remember, though, is less-complicated weapons are best. The more moving parts involved, the greater the chances of failure when the chips are down. Simple is best.

CHAPTER 9
FORCE MULTIPLIERS

Force multipliers are devices or tactics that allow you and your group to be far more effective against intruders than they might otherwise be. For example, while you're hunkered down, a video camera will allow you to see one area of your yard while anywhere from a few hundred yards to hundreds of miles away. An alarm system of some sort will let you know if someone enters your home while you're away. Traps of one kind or another will help protect certain areas when you can't be there.

Force multipliers are a poor substitute for trained personnel. But few of us have a group of several dozen highly trained and heavily armed people ready and willing to go toe to toe with all potential aggressors. Therefore, we need to stretch our resources as best we can.

Bear in mind, too, that I'm not limiting the discussion to some sort of post-collapse environment. While surveillance cameras and alarm systems won't be operational in the absence of electrical power, they are certainly useful until such a major event takes place.

ALARMS

Obviously, alarms of any sort, along with the surveillance equipment I'll discuss next, won't physically stop someone from entering your property. But they can be strong deterrents to most thieves. In fact, many convicted burglars have said that the actual or perceived presence of an alarm system was enough to cause them to move on to an easier target.

The idea behind an alarm system should be obvious: to let you know when someone enters an area without your permission. This could be a closet, an outbuilding, or even your driveway. Just about all alarms, save for a few low-budget ones you can make yourself, will require electricity. Many also have battery backups in the event of a power outage.

The alarm, once triggered, will give you a heads up that something is amiss, allowing you to take action as necessary. In some cases, that might require an armed response. Other circumstances might call for a wait-and-see approach. In the event of a burglary, an audible alarm can often be all that is necessary for them to hit the bricks.

There are numerous products available for alarming doors and windows. You can even find options at the dollar store that actually work somewhat well. An alarm I particularly like, for ease of set up, portability, and effectiveness, is the Brite-Strike Camp Alert Perimeter Security System and Survival Signaling System. It is small, about the size of a thick butane lighter, and emits a screeching 135 decibels when triggered. How loud is 135 decibels? That's only 5 decibels quieter than a jet engine sitting 100 feet away from you. The alarm is activated by the removal of a small pin in the side of the unit. The pin can be attached to a trip wire stretched across a doorway. Or, a string could be run from the pin to a door in such a way that when the door is opened, the pin is pulled.

Many of the larger home improvement stores carry DIY alarm systems. For around $150, you can get a couple of door/window sensors, a motion sensor, and a hub that will allow you to control the system remotely via your smartphone. I suggest you shop around and find a system that will allow you to expand and add additional sensors as needed.

The old standby of putting a few small stones in an empty soda can and leaving it where it will be knocked over by an intruder still works. A variation on that is to use an obnoxiously loud wind chime. Hang it on the back of your front door when you head to bed at night. If someone manages to open the door, the chime will sound. If you have cats, be sure to hang the chime high enough that it is out of reach. During the holiday season, swap the chime for a string of sleigh bells, if you'd like.

Personally, I tend to favor alarms of the four-legged variety. Dogs will smell an intruder from a far distance away. They can be trained to alert you in many ways, not just barking their fool heads off. Properly treated and cared for, you'll not find a more loyal companion nor a better alert system.

SURVEILLANCE CAMERAS

Camera systems have come a long way. They used to be large, bulky, ugly affairs with poor picture resolution. You wouldn't know if you were looking at a burglar or if a bird had defecated on the lens. With today's cameras, you could probably count the pores on the person's nose. Not to mention, cameras have gotten small enough that you can hide them just about anywhere.

If you want to go the camera route, give serious thought to investing in wireless models that utilize a Wi-Fi connection. That way, you can monitor the cameras from anywhere you have an Internet connection. Install them where you want them, such as your front hallway, your back door, and your garage, monitoring them via an app downloaded and installed on your smartphone. The cameras are motion-activated. When motion is detected, an alert will be sent to your phone. You can then watch the activity in real time and make a decision on how to proceed, such as calling the police or calling home to find out why your teenager isn't in school.

I also suggest you opt for devices that will record the footage, either on an SD card or by transmitting to a digital recorder. This way, you have evidence of the break-in, should you need it. Night vision capability is a nice feature, too.

Two great sources for camera equipment are TBO-Tech (www.TBOTech.com) and Super Circuits (www.Super Circuits.com). Both have numerous options available to suit most, if not all, your surveillance needs. There are all sorts of options for hidden cameras disguised as household objects, such as smoke detectors, clocks, DVD players, and even fake plants.

For those with a little money to spend and the time to practice flying them, drones equipped with cameras are an excellent option. They do require power, of course, and could be easily

A surveillance camera can be attached to a drone.

shot down. But, they could also provide you with much-needed information on the attacking force.

BOOBY TRAPS

Right up front, I can tell you that booby traps aren't a great idea. The trap has no way to differentiate between an intruder, a stray dog, or your grandson. It will activate or operate as designed, no matter who or what is in the vicinity. More than one person has been injured or killed by devices of their own design.

Furthermore, the legality of booby traps varies widely from state to state. In some areas, if the person was indeed trespassing, the law figures it is their own fault for getting injured. On the other hand, other locales have a very different opinion and the person who set the trap may be held liable for any and all injuries suffered by the victim, whether they were trespassing or not.

Suffice it to say, I would only suggest the use of booby traps in very limited circumstances. Having no doubt that every person in your group will remember the exact location and nature of each trap that is set, even under pressure, is qualification number one. The next qualification is legality of setting such traps in your area. It makes little sense to foil a burglary only to lose all of your assets in a forthcoming lawsuit and criminal proceedings.

Keep in mind, though, that not all booby traps need to cause injury or death. You could incorporate an alarm of some sort instead. For example, let's say you have a few small outbuildings on your property. The space behind them could make for an obvious route for an intruder to take. While you could set up some trip wires, a more clever approach would be to place a few large branches in spots where they block the path but would be easy to move. Then, wire those branches to an alarm. Of course, replacing the alarm with a small explosive charge might be preferable in a post-collapse world.

Explosives

One of my personal favorites for these purposes is black powder. It is still fairly easy to obtain through hunting stores as well as online. What I like about it is that it will ignite with an electrical charge. I can tell you from the experience of a misspent youth that a small perfume bottle filled with black powder and wired to a lantern battery will completely annihilate a wooden mailbox.

For such homemade devices, think in terms of a basic electrical circuit. A wire runs from the positive terminal of the battery to the device. Another wire goes from the device to a trigger mechanism. A third wire goes from the trigger to the negative terminal of the battery. If you're using black powder, bare wire must make contact with the powder. In the case of our exploding mailbox, we just removed the plastic coating from about a half-inch section of the wire and stuffed that bare part down into the powder.

A very simple trigger can be made using a spring clothespin and metal thumbtacks. Push the thumbtacks into the jaws of the clothespin so that when it closes, the thumbtacks make contact with one another. Place a flat piece of plastic or rubber in the jaws between the thumbtacks. Then, run your wires from those thumbtacks out to the battery and device. Attach that piece of plastic to a trip wire and when it is yanked free, the circuit is completed.

An easy and safe way to test your circuit to ensure proper operation is to replace the device with a small flashlight bulb. If the bulb lights, the circuit is complete. This is a far better option than risking having your device blow up in your face as you monkey around with the wires.

Spike Strips

Of course, there are other booby traps besides those using explosives. The spike strip is an easy one to make and can be rather useful to stop intruding vehicles. Take a long board, such as a 2x4, and pound nails through it all along the length. Space the nails about 3 inches or so apart. The nails themselves should extend beyond the board at least a few inches. The length of the board is dictated by the intended use of the spike strip. If the object is to slow or stop vehicles, the strip should be at least the width of the driveway or roadway where it will be placed. Of course, it should be disguised or hidden in some way, if at all possible.

Think outside the box. Spike strips are just as effective against people as they are against vehicles. If you have areas of your property, such as behind an outbuilding, that seem tailor-made for an attacker to sit and observe you, hiding a couple of spike strips in the weeds could be a good wake-up call for them. If you lack the boards and nails, even just broken glass and pieces of jagged metal will work.

Fish Hooks

Rumor has it that those engaged in the practice of producing illegal drugs will protect their crops by hanging fishhooks from branches at eye level. I can't imagine any group proceeding at a high rate of speed after the first of their members gets snagged.

One of the primary uses of booby traps isn't so much to eliminate the enemy, but rather to cause them to slow down their forward movement, giving you time to take action as necessary. A well-placed trap can take a few of their guys off the playing field, which is always a plus when dealing with a group of attackers. The intent of the booby trap, though, is to delay the attackers while they not only deal with their injured, but are forced to slow down to examine their route and watch for additional surprises.

AREA DENIAL

The idea behind area denial is to force attackers into locations where you can more easily deal with them. While booby traps can serve this purpose, there are other methods of area denial that aren't truly traps of any kind.

Some plants can be great for area denial. Invest in some hawthorn shrubs and plant them where you don't want people hanging out or coming through to your property. They have very long, *extremely* sharp thorns. If someone were to try to make their way through the hedge, the person behind them will definitely think twice.

Motion-activated lights are a great investment, both as a general deterrent as well as for area denial. If someone is trying to sneak up and the light goes on, they'll beat feet somewhere else. If you've planned ahead and installed fences, hedges, and such, you can, to a large degree, control where they flee, funneling them where you want. Naturally, this only works when the power is on, but why give up on such an easy solution just because there *might* come a time when electricity is an issue?

Piles of junk and garbage can serve the purpose, too. Few will want to climb over bags of stinky refuse if there appears to be a better option available. Remember, people will generally choose the path or route that looks easiest.

• • •

Force multipliers serve two purposes. First, they increase the effectiveness and efficiency of your group's defenses. Second, they allow you to be in two places at once. However, none of the suggestions in this chapter are meant to take the place of proper training and experience. Get familiar with your weapons and other resources. Drill and practice, both alone and with your group, until you reach a point where your actions and reactions are reflex.

FINAL THOUGHTS

The decision to take up arms against another person is not one to be made lightly. Intentionally harming another person, even in self-defense, can be difficult for some people to stomach. Taking a life will haunt you, to one degree or another, to the end of your days.

Understand that if you decide to arm yourself, you must do so with absolute conviction. Anything less and the other person will sense this and use that knowledge to their advantage. They will take your weapon away from you and use it against you. You need to come to terms with the thought that you may have to visit injury, and perhaps death, onto another person in order to preserve your life and the lives of your family.

Many keyboard warriors, a number of them graduates of "YouTube University," are confident of their abilities and state of mind, provided reality never truly pays them a visit. They talk a good game, full of bluster and bravado. But when push comes to shove or threat comes to action, they'll falter and fail. Only those who have put in the sweat equity, who have drilled and practiced, who have developed the blisters and, later, the callouses, are the ones who are going to succeed and prevail.

I truly and sincerely hope none of you will ever be put to the test and have to use your knowledge and training in the real world. If the need arises, I hope your skills and knowledge allow you to overcome any and all those who would do you harm.

RESOURCES

Brite-Strike

www.Brite-Strike.com

Brite-Strike was founded by two police officers who wanted
to offer better illumination products than they were finding
on the market. They are consistently ahead of the competition
when it comes to technology and manufacturing. They also
offer a couple of different personal alarm systems that are
highly recommended. I love their Camp Alert Perimeter
Security System and Survival Signaling System.

CRKT

www.CRKT.com

Columbia River Knife and Tool (CRKT) has been around
since 1994. They've made quite a name for themselves with
innovative blade designs that stand up to daily use. They have
a ton of different knives and tools to meet your needs.

KA-BAR

www.KABAR.com

KA-BAR has been making high-quality knives since the late
1800s. Their United States Marine Corps (USMC) fighting
knife in many ways set the standard for the modern fighting
knife.

Mike Parker Bows

www.mikeparkerbows.com

Mike is one of the best bowyers I've ever met. Located in Illinois, Mike makes each bow by hand to exacting standards.

Panteao Productions

www.Panteao.com

A leader in the video training world, Panteao Productions has dozens of DVDs that bring some of the world's best weapons instructors right into your living room. The videos cover innumerable firearms as well as blade fighting. The company even has a line of prepper/survival videos called Make Ready to Survive. Full disclosure, I'm one of the instructors in that series.

Steel Will Knives

www.SteelWillKnives.com

Established in 2008, Steel Will Knives is a division of Sportsman Manufacturing Group (SMG Inc.). I've found their knives to be top notch. Very well made, durable, and comfortable to use. Their Darkangel knife is my favorite tactical blade.

Streamlight

www.Streamlight.com

Streamlight has been around for over four decades now and is still going strong. Their tactical flashlights are robust, bright, and easy to use. I'm a huge fan of their ProTac 1AAA flashlight. I've used it so much I've worn away the logo on the side of it.

CREDITS

Photos by Jim Cobb

page 32, flashlights
page 97, fixed and folding knives
page 100, Kershaw Thermite and Steel Will Apostate
page 101, Emerson wave
page 102, folding knives
page 103, butterfly knife
page 105, Steel Will Darkangel
page 106, push knife
page 107, drop point knife
page 107, straight back blade
page 108, clip point bowie knife
page 109, lanyard
page 110, CRKT Sting and CRKT Synergist
page 111, Steel Will Adept 1000
page 122, baseball bat in car
page 123, sjambok
page 128, tomahawk
page 151, slungshot

Photos by Bob Hrodey

page 51, 380 pocket pistol
page 57, snub nose revolver
page 60, Glock 30
page 68, Bushmaster Carbine
page 73, pump action shotgun

Photos by Sean Neeld

page 110, tanto blades

Photos from shutterstock.com

page 7, crowd, Christian Mueller
page 8, shooting, JazzyGeoff
page 24, pepper spray, Tatiana Popova
page 28, stun gun, cosma
page 30, Taser, Kbiros
page 35, zip ties, imagedb.com
page 59, revolver, Ungnoi Lookjeab
page 61, magazine, Chris Alleaume
page 62, handgun with slide open, Looker Studio
page 64, bolt-action rifle, Guy J. Sagi
page 66, lever-action rifle, Guy J. Sagi
page 69, AR-15, Guy J. Sagi
page 70, AK-47, mashurov
page 70, sub machine gun, Militarist
page 74, shotgun, rodimov
page 81, longbow, Gyvafoto
page 82, recurve bow, Christian Weber
page 83, compound bow, Jeffrey B. Banke
page 89, crossbow, Maffi
page 92, sling shot, Coprid
page 120, brass knuckles, Chaowalit Seeneha
page 121, baton, Grushin
page 125, cane sword, Chanawat Phadwichit
page 126, machete, robtek
page 129, karambit, suwatpatt
page 134, bo staff, Michael Macsuga
page 136, nunchaku, SeDmi
page 137, tonfa, MyImages-Micha
page 138, kubotan, Depth
page 139, shuriken, Baiajaku
page 147, molotov cocktail, fotostoker
page 159, drone, Newnow

INDEX

ACKNOWLEDGMENTS

As always, first and foremost I need to thank my long-suffering wife. She puts up with my nonsense and shenanigans on a daily basis and I don't know how. I love you, Sweetheart. To my boys, keep up the good work. I'm very proud of each of you.

Special thanks to Stevie Janke for sharing her archery wisdom. I wish you all the best, my friend.

Special thanks also to Bob Hrodey for his help with photos and advice. Appreciate all you've done for me, sir.

Special thanks as well to Sean Neeld for his quick help with a few photos as well as for doing a great job moderating my Survival Weekly Facebook group.

To those of you who have tuned in to my online show at AroundtheCabin.com, I hope you've had as much with it as I have had. It is a blast getting to hang out with you folks.

Most of all, I need to thank you, the reader. It is because of your support over the last few years that I'm able to earn a living doing something I love. I appreciate that so much.

ABOUT THE AUTHOR

Jim Cobb is the author of several books focused on disaster readiness, such as *Prepper's Long-Term Survival Guide, Countdown to Preparedness, Prepper's Financial Guide,* and the #1 Amazon bestselling *Prepper's Home Defense.* He has been a student of survivalism and prepping for about 30 years. He is the owner of SurvivalWeekly.com, a rather popular disaster readiness resource. Jim and his family reside in the upper Midwest and he is currently working on several more books.